WREATHS
from the Garden

WREATHS
from the Garden

75 FRESH & DRIED FLORAL WREATHS TO MAKE

Leslie Dierks

A Sterling/Lark Book
Sterling Publishing Co., Inc.   New York

To Dorothy Grommet, whose love of flowers has been my inspiration.

Design: Dana Irwin
Photography: Evan Bracken
Production: Elaine Thompson

Library of Congress Cataloging-in-Publication Data
Dierks, Leslie.
    Wreaths from the garden : 75 fresh and dried floral wreaths
to make / Leslie Dierks.
        p.   cm.
    "A Sterling/Lark book."
    Includes index.
    ISBN 0-8069-0604-9
    1. Wreaths.   2. Flower arrangement.   3. Dried flower
arrangement.   I. Title.
SB449.5.W74D533
745.9'23--dc20   93-40711
                                                                              CIP

10 9 8 7 6 5 4 3 2 1

A Sterling/Lark Book

First paperback edition published in 1995 by
Sterling Publishing Company, Inc.
    387 Park Avenue South, New York, N.Y. 10016

Produced by Altamont Press, Inc.
    50 College Street, Asheville, NC 28801

© 1994 by Altamont Press

Distributed in Canada by Sterling Publishing
℅ Canadian Manda Group, One Atlantic Avenue, Suite 105
    Toronto, Ontario, Canada M6K 3E7
Distributed in Great Britain and Europe by Cassell PLC
    Villiers House, 41/47 Strand, London WC2N 5JE, England
Distributed in Australia by Capricorn Link (Australia) Pty Ltd.
    P.O. Box 6651, Baulkham Hills, Business Centre, NSW 2153, Australia

Sterling ISBN 0-8069-0604-9 Trade
              0-8069-0605-7 Paper

C O N T E N T S

Floral Wreaths
from Every Corner of the Garden

INTRODUCTION

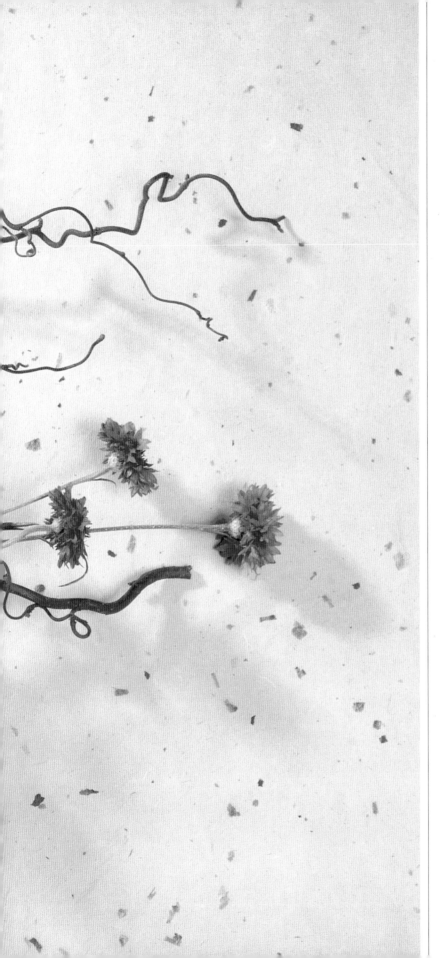

FOR MANY PEOPLE, *there is a special place reserved in the heart for flowers. As I grew up, I often watched my mother as she puttered in her garden. She could spend hours there every day during the summer, caring less about the dirt under her fingernails than about the condition of her flowers. She doted upon them at each stage of development, from encouraging the emerging shoots to mulching-in the spent plants. Hearing her detail the virtues of each species, I soon acquired an undying appreciation for these most splendid of nature's miracles.*

Others have shared this appreciation for centuries, and a love of flowers crosses all cultural and political boundaries. Once humanity evolved beyond the need to view every living thing in terms of its food value, flowers were recognized for their beauty alone. And that beauty has enhanced human existence in countless ways ever since.

Flowers have made their way into our homes in ways both obvious and subtle. A freshly picked bouquet enlivens a kitchen table for several days, and a treasured Persian rug with its floral motif is enjoyed for generations. The decorative properties of flowers have been applied to everything from walls to soap dishes.

One of the best ways we can use flowers is to make them into wreaths. To do so is to continue a long tradition of weaving flowers into circular forms, and while the earliest examples were applied for their healing or other spiritual properties, we can enjoy our own wreaths purely for their aesthetic value. Whether fresh or dried (or perhaps a combination of the two), floral wreaths are some of the most beautiful and most natural embellishments we can add to our lives.

9

F R E S H
F L O W E R S

*For the most spectacular of floral
wreaths, choose fresh materials.
The results of your efforts
may last only a few days,
but what a glorious display
they will make!*

G R O W I N G
Y O U R   O W N

In recent years, gardening has become almost a passion for
many who live and work in otherwise high stress, high tech
environments. You don't need a country estate or horticultural degree to produce lovely blossoms. If you have just a tiny
patch of soil—even a window box will do—and a moderate
interest in the outcome, you can be a successful gardener.

Many flowers can be grown from seeds that are widely
available from mail-order catalogs, plant nurseries, and
discount stores. Some plants, however, have rather compli-
cated requirements that must be met for them to germinate
and prosper. An easier approach is to purchase small plants
that are already well established and can be readily trans-
planted into your own soil.

Plants, like people, have preferences and habits that you'll
be wise to respect. Most flowers prefer sunlight to shade,
but some prefer the protection of a tree branch overhead
and will shrivel and burn with too much sun. While adequate moisture and food are essential, too much can be just

11

as harmful as too little. Above all, good drainage is a must for any garden, especially those that are container-bound.

Entire libraries have been written about how to cultivate flowering plants, and ready-made plans exist for any "look" you want, from the relative clutter of an English cottage garden to the more austere designs of the Japanese. Don't let all that expertise confuse and overwhelm you, though; nothing works better than digging your own fingers into the soil and learning firsthand from your successes and your mistakes.

OTHER SOURCES OF FLOWERS

If you have neither the time nor the inclination to grow your own, there are many other sources of fresh blooms. Florist shops carry the widest variety, and they can probably order any particular flowers you may desire. Other alternatives include grocery stores, produce markets, farm stands, and street vendors. While more limited in their selections, these sources offer colorful, mixed bouquets at very reasonable prices.

Wildflowers growing in a vacant lot or along a country road make beautiful fresh wreaths, and many varieties also dry quite successfully. If you find these native plants irresistible, please remember a few golden rules of picking flowers: always ask permission of the property owner, leave plenty to go to seed to ensure next year's crop, and never dig up a wildflower. Many native plants are becoming endangered due to overzealous collectors. And if you're tempted to pull over on an interstate to take advantage of the landscaping efforts of your state's transportation department, keep in mind that most state troopers don't consider flower picking to be an "emergency" that warrants stopping.

CUTTING FLOWERS

Cut fresh flowers for your wreaths when they are at their peak of perfection—in the early morning hours or late in the evening. Bring a container of warm water with you into the garden so that you can immerse the stems immediately after you cut them. If you don't have a pair of very sharp scissors, use a knife instead. No matter what tools you use, make sure they are clean because the bacteria on a dirty knife or bucket will multiply and restrict the flow of water into the stems. Cut the stems at an angle for better water absorption, and remove any foliage below the water level.

To prolong the life of your flowers, add a preservative to the water, and set your flowers in a cool, dark room for six to eight hours. The combination of warm water and cool air conditions the flowers and makes them firmer. Commercial preservatives are available from local florists, but you can make your own by adding one tablespoon each of bleach and sugar to a gallon of water. An alternative recipe is a gallon of water mixed with two tablespoons of medicinal mouthwash and 12 ounces of a clear soft drink. The added sugar provides energy to the plant, while the other ingredients (bleach or bactericide) help deter the growth of microorganisms that clog the stems.

Flowers with woody stems should have the bottom of the stems mashed or split. Split the stems of roses by making lengthwise cuts with a sharp knife. Other woody-stemmed flowers should receive a well-placed hammer blow to the bottom inch or two (2.5 to 5 cm) of the stem. For those with a milky sap, seal the end of the stems with a match flame to prevent the loss of fluid.

Once you've conditioned your blooms and arranged them into a wreath, you may want to use a preservative spray to help prevent the flowers from losing moisture through their petals.

Commercial preparations such as Crowning Glory or Clear Set are commonly used by florists. A similar, home-made solution consists of one part clear acrylic floor wax mixed with four parts water. Spritz the preservative onto any flower with dense, solid petals.

For longer lasting fresh wreaths, keep them out of the rays of the hot sun. Periodically check their water supply, and give them an occasional misting to help keep them looking perky. Aside from prematurely aging your flowers, sunlight can have other unintended consequences. Even after having been cut, some blossoms (tulips, for example) are notorious for turning their faces toward the light.

13

DRIED FLOWERS

*Fortunately, for those of us who want our wreaths to last longer than this weekend's family reunion, there are several methods for preserving flowers.
Dried flowers are quite popular and widely available at craft shops, floral shops, and farmers' markets, and it's easy and fun to make your own.*

❖

AIR DRYING

By far the simplest method of preserving flowers is to hang them in clusters, heads facing down, and allow them to air dry. You have only a few conditions to satisfy in order to produce good results: low light levels, good air circulation, and low humidity. Exposure to sunlight will fade the colors of darker flowers, and stagnant, moist air will cause mold and mildew to develop.

Collect your flowers to be dried, and strip off the larger foliage. Most leaves curl beyond recognition and are extremely brittle when they dry. In fact, the smaller leaves will crumble when you handle the dried stems. Gather similar flowers into small bunches, securing the bottoms of the stems with rubber bands. Rubber bands are superior to string or wire because as the stems shrink, the bands will compress and continue to hold the flowers together.

The length of time required for flowers to dry completely depends upon the variety of flower, size of your bunches, 15

and the surrounding conditions. After a few days, test your blooms for doneness by carefully touching the thickest part of the flower head and by bending one of the stems. The flower head should feel dry, almost papery, and the stem should snap neatly. When testing, be sure to check the flowers in the center of each cluster, as these generally dry the slowest.

DESICCANTS

The use of a desiccant—a material that absorbs moisture—can produce dried flowers with exceptional color and form. The only drawback is that the finished materials must be handled with great care due to their brittleness. Of the most commonly used substances, silica gel is by far the best. While a bit more expensive than alternatives such as sand or borax, it is much more effective at drawing out moisture.

When drying flowers with a desiccant, trim the stems to about an inch (2.5 cm) in length. Spread a layer of silica gel about one inch (2.5 cm) deep in your container, and position your flowers so they're not touching each other. Then carefully add crystals all around and inside the flowers, eventually covering them completely. Place a tight lid on your container (or set it inside a plastic bag if it has no lid), and store it in a warm place.

Check your flowers for dryness after about 48 hours. Drying times vary, but don't leave your flowers in too long or they will fall apart. When uncovering your blossoms, it pays to use an archaeologist's approach. A small artist's brush is a gentler tool to remove excess crystals than a finger or a spoon.

For flowers with dense centers such as roses and carnations, remove the blossoms when the petals first feel dry. Then reinsert the stem of each flower into the silica gel so that the petals are not quite touching the crystals. Replace the lid, and allow the flowers to sit for another two to four days. The additional time will dry the thicker center without ruining the petals.

One major advantage to silica gel is that you can use it indefinitely. Most crystals change color when they are fully laden with moisture, and you can rejuvenate them by placing them in a warm oven or a microwave until they return to their original tint.

GLYCERINE

Another quite different technique is to use a solution of glycerine and water to replace the plant's natural moisture rather than eliminate it. This method is most often used for foliage, which is often too brittle when dried by air or with a desiccant.

Although some people recommend a one-to-one solution, generally one part glycerine to two parts water is sufficient. The water should be quite hot—near boiling—and the solution mixed thoroughly to keep it from separating. Before immersing the plants, allow the solution to cool until it's no longer hot to the touch.

When cutting plants for this purpose, choose mature specimens; new growth doesn't absorb the preservative very well. If you've cut the plants some time prior to mixing the glycerine solution, recut the stems, making sure to batter any woody stems.

Depending on the thickness and texture of the foliage, the process can take anywhere from a few days to a few weeks. When all of the leaves have experienced a shift in color, the plant has absorbed enough of the glycerine. The finished leaves also feel smooth and supple. If you detect small droplets of glycerine on the leaves, remove the branch and rinse it off. Too much glycerine can encourage the growth of mold and mildew.

The final color varies according to the plant, and you can influence the outcome somewhat by altering the light level. Generally, the best color is achieved by keeping the foliage in the dark throughout the process.

W R E A T H
M A K I N G

T O O L S   A N D
M A T E R I A L S

*Very little equipment is necessary
to make a floral wreath: just a
wreath base and the means to
attach your flowers to it.*

B A S E S

*Most discount stores now carry an assortment of the more
common wreath bases. For something more unusual, try craft
shops, florists, and garden supply stores. When you make
your selection, keep in mind the look you want to achieve.*

*A traditional straw base generally produces a full, fluffy-
looking wreath; the wreath made with Joe-Pye weed shown
on page 91 is a good example of this type. These bases are
quite bulky, and they are usually completely covered with
floral materials because the straw itself is not very attractive.*

*Probably the least expensive base you can find is one made
of plastic foam. Light in weight and surprisingly sturdy, foam
is even homelier than straw. This material too should be fully
covered by your materials. A good way to start is to wrap a
foam base with sheet moss or ribbon to disguise it.*

*If you have plenty of background materials, a wire ring
makes a wonderfully delicate-looking wreath. The heart-
shaped baby's-breath wreath on page 28 is made on a wire
base that is covered with scrap pieces of silver king
artemisia. For an altogether different effect, attach* 19

preserved greens to your ring. The ammobium wreath on page 71 is built with glycerine-preserved ferns.

You can also buy wreath bases covered entirely in Spanish moss. This is a soft, pliable material that generally complements the flowers and foliage you place on top. The statice wreath on page 68 sits on such a base.

The greatest variety can be found in bases made of vines. In addition to traditional ovals and circles, you can find basket shapes, flat woven hearts, and all manner of abstract forms. Depending on the type of vine used, these bases can be bulky or dainty in appearance. Vine bases are often so handsome you'll want to leave portions exposed to view. There are numerous examples in the following pages where the form of the base has been incorporated into the design of the wreath.

For a wreath that demonstrates nature's exuberance, choose one of the many available bases made from twigs. Great spinning whorls of branches from willow or beech trees make delightful backgrounds for colorful arrangements of flowers.

To keep your freshly cut blossoms bright and cheerful, the easiest base to use is one made entirely of floral oasis. This is a dense plastic foam, usually green, that can be saturated with water. Most oasis bases have a plastic backing that prevents the moisture from ruining the surface on which it is set—probably your dining room table or other fine furniture. If you can't find one ready-made in your local craft shop, you can create the same effect by cutting blocks of oasis and taping or wiring them onto a multi-ringed wire base. You can buy thin floral tape intended for this purpose. With your homemade version, be sure to place a piece of glass or plexiglass under your wreath, or it will leave a water mark on your furniture.

If you love vine or twig bases and want to use fresh flowers, don't despair. You can put your moisture where you need it by inserting your flowers first into floral tubes—small plastic vials that hold a small amount of water—then into the base. Keep in mind that the amount of water these tubes will hold is very skimpy. A thirsty stem can drink the entire contents in just a few hours.

A better choice, especially for multiple flowers, is to use a caged oasis or a bouquet holder minus the handle. The former is available mainly through floral suppliers, but you can find the latter at craft shops. One or more can be wired or hot-glued to the base to contain enough moisture to satisfy several blooms.

Another way to display fresh flowers in a wreath is to include the entire living plant. The cyclamen in the wreath on page 51 is planted in a small basket wired to the base. An alternative method that allows the use of small plants around the entire wreath is to use a wire cage base. Lined with sphagnum moss, this type of base will hold enough soil for a number of small plants.

MAKING THE ATTACHMENT

A medley of tools exists to help hold your flowers onto your wreaths. Depending on which base you choose, and your own style of working, you'll soon discover those you prefer. It is in this respect that fresh flowers have an advantage over dried ones—usually their stems are strong enough to hold them in place without any additional assistance.

Floral picks are your best bet when you have slender, delicate stems to insert. These slivers of wood are sharply pointed at one end and have a fine wire attached at the other. Simply make a small cluster of blossoms or leaves, and break the stems so they are about two-thirds the length of the pick. Then grasp the stems alongside the pick, and spiral the wire around both together.

Wire is another invaluable tool. At the very least, it can be used to fashion a hanger by which you can display your creation. Often wire is used to attach clusters of herbs or flowers to a wire ring, but it can also be used the same way with vine and straw bases. Regular wire works fine, but floral wire, which is painted green, is less obtrusive.

Substitutes for wire include monofilament (fishing line) and yarn. Some designers prefer the near invisibility of the monofilament or the soft flexibility of the yarn. You decide which works best.

Saving the best for last, the handiest tool in the wreath maker's arsenal is the glue gun. While not appropriate for fresh flowers, it is ideal for attaching dried materials, pieces of sheet moss, and innumerable embellishments. It's simple to use and produces a strong, nearly invisible bond. Insert a stick of glue, plug in the gun, and when it has reached temperature, just point and "fire" a bit of melted glue onto the stems or back of your flower cluster. After you've held the material in place for several seconds, it's secure.

As with any electric tool, there are a few cautions you should observe. Both the tip of the gun and the glue it extrudes get quite hot. They can melt small holes into a foam base, damage fresh flowers, and burn your fingers. For those less daring, there are also warm-melt glue guns available. Whichever version you select, never leave a child alone with a glue gun.

For a more finished appearance (and greater security if you plan to keep your wreath for a long time) wrap the wired portion of your picked cluster with floral tape. Apply this slightly sticky tape by lightly stretching it as you wrap. When pressed together, the tape will adhere to itself.

One neat trick to do with floral tape is to twist it tightly into a string. This is strong yet gentle enough to hold a fresh stem in place against a vine wreath. When tied onto the vine, the tape's twisted, curly ends look almost like part of the vine.

Floral pins, those silver U-shaped devices with zigzags across the top, are great for securing Spanish moss or individual leaves to a straw, foam, or oasis base.

PERENNIALS

PLANTING PERENNIALS *is the gardening equivalent to investing in blue-chip stocks: your initial investment grows and multiplies, and you receive dividends in the form of flowers every year. Most are easy to grow and, once established, they often thrive despite considerable neglect.*

The secret to the longevity of perennials lies in their roots. Annuals emerge from seed, blossom, and produce new seed all in a single year to assure their reproduction. Perennials thrive and multiply by devoting their energy to maintaining a viable root system. While the stems and foliage generally die back during the cold months, the roots remain alive by becoming dormant. Some such as creeping phlox and candytuft (whose Latin name, Iberis sempervirens, means Spanish evergreen) are hardy enough to retain their leaves throughout the winter.

The dependability and longevity of a perennial are offset by the short life span of its flowers. Few last longer than a month, and the most dramatic ones bloom for an even shorter period. Luckily, there are hundreds of species of perennials, more than enough to span the entire growing season.

Starting off the year, warm spring breezes bring forth such old-fashioned favorites as the brilliant, ground-hugging primrose and the tall, graceful columbine. As the days lengthen into summer, peonies spread their exuberance, coralbells ring a colorful chorus, and delphiniums raise their stately spires. In the heat of summer's dog days, baby's-breath raises a cloud of tiny white blossoms, and sweet-scented bee balm attracts swarms of butterflies. Cooler fall nights are accompanied by a blast of form and color in the blooms of chrysanthemums and hardy asters. In winter, when flowers of any sort are rare, the blossoms of the Christmas rose echo the purest white of freshly fallen snow.*

If you would like to try growing perennials from seed, you'll do well to remember that they are slower to germinate than annuals or vegetables. In fact, the seeds of some perennials—Christmas rose and peony, for example—take more than a year to sprout. You're better off to buy these as potted plants. Most don't flower in their first year; the plant spends its first growing season establishing a sturdy root system and foliage to support a greater profusion of flowers later. Some of the easiest perennials to grow from seeds include foxglove, coralbells, delphinium, and primrose.

One of the best ways to obtain more perennials is to divide existing plants. Gardening friends are often eager to share plants this way, and the plants themselves will benefit from the process. Perennials are rejuvenated when they are dug every three or four years and the rootstock divided into several smaller clumps. For dividing spring blooming plants, fall is the best time, and late bloomers can be divided in the spring.

FOR SUMPTUOUSNESS, *nothing can quite match the peony (Paeonia). Its ruffled flowers have more petals than Scarlet O'Hara had petticoats, and the blossoms range in color from a creamy French vanilla to deep burgundy, with numerous shades of pink and mauve in between.*

Although these blooms look as if they are freshly cut from the garden, they are actually freeze-dried, a process that preserves their full beauty of form and color. (It is not a process you should attempt at home, however. Flowers placed in a home freezer are destined to become a soggy mass.) Here the glorious blooms are resting on a bed of redolent mountain mint and tips of baby's-breath, both of which are glued to a flat wreath made of curved vines. Loops of lace over grosgrain ribbon alternate with the blossoms and tie the color scheme together. (Hint: Use two separate pieces of ribbon to make the double loops, and attach them together with hot glue.)

A DELIGHT FOR BEES, *hummingbirds, and children who love to sip nectar, honeysuckle (Lonicera) is a remarkably undemanding plant. It is a perennial vine that flourishes even in poor soil. When not in bloom, the vine itself makes beautiful wreath bases that are much more delicate looking than those made with grapevines. Honeysuckle is easily trained to grow up a trellis, but if you live in a southerly climate, beware! Once established, this fragrant flower can easily become invasive.*

Because it is a vine, honeysuckle offers its own, ready-made base. Select a half-dozen attractive pieces of vine, each about two to three feet (.6 to .9 m) in length. Without breaking off the flowers and leaves, loosely twine the lengths together into a circle. Then add a ribbon accent to hold the vines together. Now cut three to five flower clusters, placing these in a floral tube filled with water. Tuck the tube into the vines at the bow, using the ribbon to hide the plastic point.

WITH ITS FLURRY of tiny flowers suspended on nearly invisible stems, baby's-breath (Gypsophila) looks like snowflakes dancing in the air. Planted in the garden, it will do well in any sunny spot that has plenty of elbow room. The double-formed flowers are the most popular variety and are equally good for cutting and for drying.

In floral arrangements, baby's-breath is most often used as an accompaniment, taking second stage to larger, showier flowers. As this charming wreath demonstrates, a mass of baby's-breath can hold its own quite nicely. You can use dried or fresh flowers (they will dry perfectly well in place) to recreate this romantic valentine. The base is a heart-shaped wire form covered with scraps of artemisia to give it some fullness. Starting at the top and ending at the point of the heart, small bouquets of baby's-breath are attached to the frame with monofilament. A bow of pink moiré ribbon with a dried rose in the center is hot-glued to the bottom.

BABY'S-BREATH IS IDEAL for a bridal corona or to wear on other special occasions. Using 22-gauge wire, measure enough to encircle the head to be adorned. Form the wire into a circle, wrapping floral tape over the joint and around the entire ring. Make a cluster of fresh baby's-breath about 1-1/2 inches (4 cm) long, and tape it onto the ring. Without breaking the tape, add another cluster so that it covers the attachment of the first. Work continuously around the ring, adding more clusters every inch or so (about every 3 cm). After working about a third of the ring, turn the wreath upside down (it gets too heavy and flops otherwise) and continue. Entwine two strands of small pearls around the wreath, and attach them at both ends with hot glue. After adding the pearls, fluff the baby's-breath to restore its fullness. Then loop a narrow ribbon around the wreath, making a knot every few inches (about every 7 cm). Make a small bow, add an extra strand of pearls at the center, and secure the combination with a chenille stem. For a romantic look, tie a "love knot" on the end of each streamer.

ASTERS BELONG TO *that confusing group of plants that straddles the line between annuals and perennials. Hardy asters, also known as Michaelmas daisies, are true perennials, while China asters last but one season. One of the longest blooming perennials, hardy asters provide masses of color from late summer through fall.*

This spectacular wreath demonstrates the wide variety among asters. The small, white Monto Casino and light blue novi-belgii blossoms at top center and bottom right, respectively, closely resemble native plants you'll find grow- ing wild in open woods and along roadsides. The larger pink, purple, and white blos- soms display the perfection of hybrids, and the tiny, starlike golden asters are unique droplets of color. To carry off the drama of the flowers, two vine bases are wired together. Then a large bouquet holder is glued and wired at the bottom center to provide moisture to the flowers. Insert all of the stems into the well-soaked oasis, and direct the blossoms into an artistic arrangement.

31

A PERENNIAL HERB *native to Europe, tansy* (Tanacetum) *is welcomed in any garden, not for its historic culinary purposes but for its usefulness as a dried flower. Its diminutive, bright yellow flowers stand on tall stems that are covered with fernlike leaves.*

To make this feathery wreath, start with a crimped wire frame covered with moss. Cut four-inch (10-cm) stems of pepper-grass, and secure them to the base with monofilament. Add texture with an assortment of other grasses glued on top. Finish the wreath with clusters of tansy buttons and single stems of yellow daisies hot-glued in place.

A WREATH BASKET *made of slender vines is filled with fragrant, golden tansy and feathery German statice. Purchase a wreath form that has the bottom half woven into a narrow opening, or fashion one of your own from honeysuckle or young, supple grapevines. Begin by wiring a peach paper ribbon bow to the top, leaving the streamers to be arranged later. After heavily misting the German statice to make it more pliable and less likely to shed, hot-glue several sprigs across the front and back of the opening. Once the white statice outline is complete, make bunches of tansy, wrapping the stems together with floral tape, and hot-glue them into the center of the basket. Finally, arrange the ribbon streamers into graceful curves along the sides, and secure them in place with dots of hot glue.*

ONE OF THE VERY FIRST FLOWERS to be cultivated in the garden is the carnation (Dianthus caryophyllus). Several varieties now exist that are hardy in areas with true winters, but many professionals agree that carnations are not easy to cultivate. Given the legion of carnation lovers who are undeterred, the allure of the flower's charming ruffles and sweet scent must be more than adequate compensation for the effort. Carnations are closely related to pinks (D. plumarius) and sweet William (D. barbatus).

A striking combination results when you mix white with shades of rose and deep, emerald green. Start with the greenery; here it is a combination of leatherleaf fern, lycopodium, and lemonleaf (the broad, flat leaves). Insert small pieces of each all around a well-soaked oasis base, making sure to alternate the greens to highlight the textural variety. Using the carnation blossoms as pinpoints of color, add about four dozen, again mixing the varieties so that each color is not concentrated in a single area. If you want the leaves to glisten as they do here, spray your wreath with a commercial preservative or with your homemade recipe (see page 13).

SOME CARNATIONS ARE *artificially "enhanced" to give them a brighter color, but these vivid blooms are completely natural. With the flower heads tucked up tightly against one another, the effect is that of an unbroken coral ring. Thoroughly soak an oasis ring, and insert the blossoms so that the petals touch each other. The stems should be cut very* short—*about one inch (2.5 cm) long—so the blooms will stand straight up. If you use these massive blossoms (the kind sold by florists), you'll need about 14 or 15 for an eight-inch ring. Finally, place bits of boxwood and misty blue or caspia around the inner and outer edges.*

THE NAME CORALBELLS (Heuchera) *perfectly describes the dainty flowers that fill the stems of this popular plant. They dangle from light, airy stems that stand as much as two feet (.6 m) above the low-growing foliage. Periodic cutting produces long-lasting fresh flowers for wreaths and bouquets, and it induces the plant to continue flowering throughout the summer.*

Wire two vine bases together to make this figure-eight wreath. With hot glue and wire, attach a moistened bouquet holder where they join. Both the wire and the edges of the bouquet holder can be hidden with clumps of Spanish moss. To create the floral composition, insert a few galax leaves and fern tips into the oasis, and add the coralbells so the flowers make an inverted triangle pattern. If desired, add a couple of stems of curly willow for accents.

THERE IS NO CLEARER BLUE in the gardener's palette than that displayed by the delphinium. Its majestic spires—sometimes as tall as six feet (nearly two meters)—are a gardener's pride and joy. Also available in pale mauve tones, brilliant white, and deep violets, delphiniums add a strong vertical component to the perennial garden.

At first glance, delphiniums appear impossible to use for wreath making. One solution, as demonstrated by this delicate wreath, is simply to clip small sections of the stems, an approach that spotlights the beauty of the individual florets. The wreath is made using a wire ring that is completely covered with dried artemisia. Next, generous bunches of caspia and white statice are tied onto the base to set the stage for the delphinium blossoms. The dried delphiniums are then hot-glued in place around the wreath, together with a few individual stems of deep blue salvia. As a final touch, a simple bow tied from velvet ribbon is secured with hot glue to the back of the wreath.

OF ALL FLOWERING PLANTS, *daisies* (Chrysanthemum) *are probably the most beloved. Their friendly faces pop up in meadows and along roadsides every season, the essence of summer's innocence. Among its cultivated varieties, the shasta daisy is probably the most familiar, but this vast family of flowers also includes chrysanthemums, coreopsis, gallardia, and the irrepressible dandelion.*

A scant assortment of materials is all you need to create this garden-fresh display. The base is a quick twist of a few cast-off stems from artificial flowers, with a bright yellow ribbon twined around it. Curl five or six stems loosely around the fingers, and entwine them together to make the base, or substitute a small, loosely woven vine wreath. To provide water to the flowers, hot-glue a small oasis holder into the base, followed by a bit of sheet moss to disguise the mechanics. Cut a dozen blooms to create a crescent-shaped array, and insert them into the small oasis with some short fern tips to conceal the stems. A small bow glued to the bottom adds a finishing touch.

WITH MORE THAN 150 SPECIES, chrysanthemums form a significant branch of the daisy family. This most popular of fall-blooming plants has a flower to please everyone. As demonstrated by this magnificent wreath, mums range in size from dainty buttons to the huge pompoms so prevalent at football games. Some have single, flat daisylike petals, and others have long, narrow tendrils that inspire the name "spider mum."

For a natural look, start with a pine needle base, and provide the necessary moisture for the flowers by gluing and wiring a bouquet holder at the bottom. Arrange the largest mums first, leaving room for several longer stems to be inserted at the top and on each side. With their ends cut to sharp points, a few branches of curly willow can be poked directly into the base in areas where a little extra texture is needed.

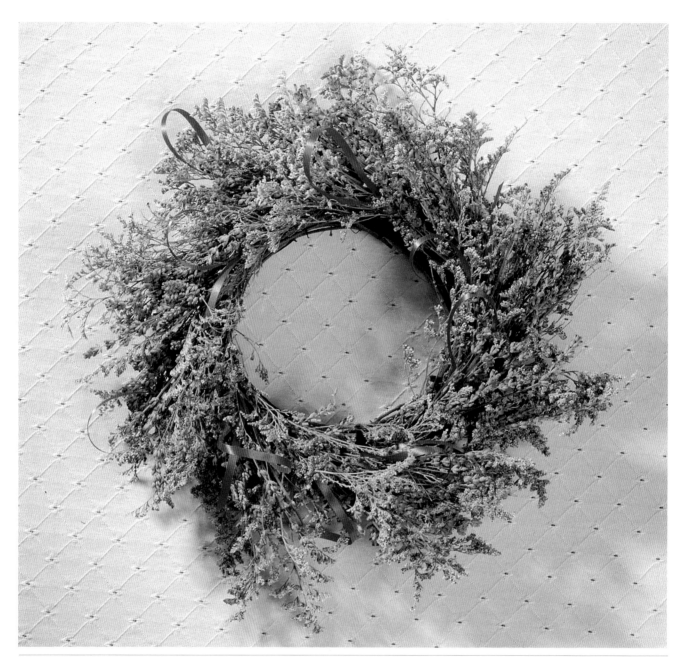

MANY OLD-FASHIONED *perennial favorites also quali-*
fy as herbs, and lavender (Lavandula) is a prime example.
Noted for its gentle, clean fragrance, lavender has long been
used for soaps, bath oil, and potpourri. A wreath made of
fresh lavender can fill an entire room with scent. When dried,
it holds nearly all its color and much of its fragrance.

To make this wreath, start with a small vine base. Cut several
short lengths of brown yarn or fine-gauge wire to use for tying
the flowers onto the vines. Then form bunches of caspia, plac-
ing about 20 to 30 lavender stems on the top of each bunch.
Moving in a single direction around the base, tie or wire the
bunches in a spiral pattern onto the wreath. Be sure to cover
the stems and wire of each bunch with the flowers of the suc-
ceeding one. Using a narrow satin ribbon in a complementary
shade of lavender, form loops, and hot-glue them randomly
around the wreath.

THERE ARE FEW PERENNIALS that are so easy to grow and so trouble-free as the veronica. Also commonly called speedwell, these tough plants are long-lived, have few pest or disease problems, and will thrive anywhere there is sun. Spires of lavender-blue, rose, and white blossoms range in height from only an inch (2.5 cm) to almost a foot (30 cm). In addition to making good cut flowers, they dry quite successfully.

In a symphony of pastels, pink and blue spikes of veronica sit atop a field of silvery green lamb's ears. Wrap a metal ring with floral tape to use for the base. Then, using fine-gauge wire, alternately add bunches of lamb's ears, small bouquets of veronica and German statice, and clusters of mountain mint. Continue around until you complete the circle. To add more touches of color, hot-glue additional veronica on top.

41

B U L B S

ONCE YOU'VE EXPERIENCED *first hand the miracle of snowdrops, crocuses, or daffodils poking their heads up through a blanket of snow to dance in the first mild breezes of early spring, you can easily understand how bulbs could become a valuable commodity of exchange. Actually the most ardent pursuit of ever more valuable bulbs—a speculative fever that dwarfed the events leading up to the stock market crash of 1929—centered around a single flower, the tulip.*

It all began in the otherwise sedate nation of Holland in the early 1600s. The tulip, a native of Turkey, had been introduced to Flemish gardeners about 20 years earlier, and it was already providing the basis for the Dutch business of growing bulbs. What sparked the extraordinary speculation in tulips was the demand for rare colors and combinations. At the time, the Flemish love for the blossoms was so intense that unusual varieties could easily fetch thousands of dollars. It soon became apparent to all that new colors and patterns in tulips can arise unpredictably from common bulbs. We now know that this is caused both by natural mutation and by a virus that can affect the plant's genetic code. But in 17th-century Holland, owning bulbs was like holding a lottery ticket. Anyone could win. When the sale of tulip bulbs evolved into the trading of bulb futures, the mania became outright madness. And, like any speculative bubble, it ultimately burst.

Today the purchase and sale of tulips and other bulbs are much less exhilarating but considerably more predictable.

They are significantly more reasonable in price, too. In fact, considering that bulbs have a self-contained store of food and a propensity to multiply, they are quite a bargain.

Approximately 3,000 species of plants are considered by gardeners to be bulbs. In truth this is more of a convenience than a scientific determination. Only about half—plants such as tulips, daffodils, and hyacinths—are true bulbs. Others are corms (freesia and crocus), tubers (begonia and anemone), tuberous roots (dahlia and winter aconite), and rhizomes (lily-of-the-valley and canna). Each type grows in a slightly different way, but they all have a built-in storehouse of food to tide them through a dormancy period and to fuel the development of the plant and flower.

Favorite spring-flowering bulbs (crocus, iris, tulip, and the like) are all planted in the fall, after much of the garden's beauty has been played out. The excitement and anticipation of new additions to next season's bounty come just at the time when this year's projects are growing wearisome. Spring bulbs are not only hardy, they require a period of cold weather to develop properly.

Summer-flowering bulbs such as the canna and the dahlia are tender and must be planted in spring after the soil has warmed. At the end of their season, they must be dug up and stored in dry, cool conditions throughout the winter before replanting the next year.

THE SEASON'S FIRST *flush of warm weather often heralds some rather unusual behavior, even among plants. Looking more like rare, tropical plants than the staid, upstanding tulips (Tulipa) they are, these golden blossoms have opened their petals in the widest possible embrace to soak up every ray of sunshine. Cut with short stems, they are arranged in a well-soaked oasis base together with a trio of* pink and yellow bicolored tulips that have been carefully opened by hand to complement their exuberant cousins. Tips of variegated ivy and fingerfuls of Spanish ivy are tucked in around the edges to hide the base and soften the edges. A narrow pink ribbon, picked in at several locations, threads its way among the flowers to tie the composition together.

W HETHER FRESH OR DRIED, *ivy runners coiled around themselves make an excellent lightweight wreath base. One approach is to make the wreath fresh and allow it to dry as it hangs. Alternatively, if you prefer the look of dried ivy with your fresh blossoms, make up your base a few weeks ahead of time. Cut the handle off a small bouquet holder, wire the holder onto the ivy base, and add some hot glue for added assurance. After covering the holder with four or five dried galax leaves, insert three tulips. Add a bow, looping the extra ribbon around the wreath. Finally, use sprigs of misty blue, leptospermum, and baby's-breath to create a cloud effect around the tulips.*

*I*RISES ARE AMONG *the most popular of bulbs, probably due to their wide range of forms and colors. All have a generally triangular symmetry, but some have wide, flat blossoms while others have long, droopy "beards"; still others display tall, slender petals. They range in height from dwarfs* (Iris reticulata) *to giants* (I. sibirica). *Their wide range of colors includes some striking combinations, lacking only a true red.*

To make a natural-looking wreath befitting your favorite irises, collect the cuttings from your shrubs when you prune them. Shape the branches shortly after they're cut, when they are most pliable. Then wire them together in a few places, and cover the wires with pieces of sheet moss. To provide moisture to your flowers, wire and hot-glue a bouquet holder in a lower corner. Next, glue a purchased bird's nest at the bottom so that it looks as if it's resting among the branches. Now insert the irises, some leatherleaf fern tips, and several yellow button chrysanthemums into the bouquet holder, positioning them in an L-shape. Into the nest, glue a few artificial eggs that have been painted a pale shade of blue.

ENOUGH CANNOT BE SAID *for the magnificence of lilies (Lilium). When planted in the garden, their color and fragrance attract scores of butterflies as well as humming-birds. As a cut flower, many will last up to a week. Just be sure to leave behind as much stem as possible when you cut them; the greenery feeds the bulb for next year's flowers.*

With lilies, it seems as if each variety is more beautiful than the last, but "Stargazer" remains a constant favorite among floral designers. Its superb color and graceful form add ele-

gance to any arrangement, but there is no doubt that its abundant freckles also have a certain appeal. In this lovely wreath, a half-dozen "Stargazer" blossoms are clustered at the top of a Spanish moss-covered oasis ring. Underneath the lilies, a handful of galax leaves, rubbed with vegetable oil to make them glisten, provide strong contrast to the creamy white edges of the flower petals. For that little something extra, a copper cord is draped around the wreath and among the flowers.

AS BRILLIANT AS GEMSTONES, *anemones are tempt-
ing but sometimes difficult for the amateur gardener. Their
hardiness varies according to the species, and you're better off
resigning yourself to setting out new tubers or rhizomes each
year. If you can approximate their native conditions, anemones
will reward you with showy blossoms in blues, purples, reds,
and pure white, all of which last several days when cut.*

*Simplicity itself, this small wreath contains no other flowers
but anemones in sparkling shades of red and purple. Cut the
short stems on an angle to ease their insertion into a well-
soaked oasis base, and arrange the flower heads to face in all
directions. Use small pinches of Spanish moss pinned into the
oasis to conceal any of the base that might show.*

ALTHOUGH SNOWDROPS AND crocuses may emerge sooner, nothing is more welcome as winter lessens its grip than the sight of the season's first daffodils (Narcissus). Their cheerful blossoms range in color from snow white to deep, buttery yellow, with combinations that include some with coral-colored trumpets.

This wreath displays two daffodil varieties against a backdrop of soft, furry lamb's ears, spikes of lavender, and pussy willows bursting into bloom. To keep them fresh, the daffodils plus a few stems of candytuft are inserted into floral tubes. (This wreath required five.) The tubes are then wired to a straw base that has been covered with lamb's ears and lavender. These can be picked or wired onto the base, but make sure to leave room for the somewhat bulky tubes. Conceal the tubes with more lavender and lamb's ears, adding the pussy willows as a final garnish along the bottom.

49

W ITH ITS EXQUISITE FRAGRANCE and tinkling white bells suspended from gently curved stems, lily-of-the-valley (Convallaria) is a delight to all the senses. It naturalizes well under trees, where it easily forms a carpet of long, oval leaves. Not a true bulb, lily-of-the-valley is grown by planting rhizomes called pips. They may be forced to bloom indoors, but to do so, the pips must first experience near-freezing temperatures for at least two months.

A study in simplicity, this wreath is made totally of lily-of-the-valley flowers and leaves. Insert the individual leaves and blossoms into a well-moistened oasis base. For the symmetrical design here, spiral the materials in a single direction around the wreath. A more casual effect can be achieved by varying the direction of the foliage and blooms.

THERE ARE TWO DISTINCT types of cyclamen: the smaller flowers native to European woodlands, and the larger, more perfect blossoms available from florists. Several species of the former type can be grown in the home garden, and many are hardy in areas where the average winter temperature doesn't drop below zero. The latter types are incredibly fussy and are probably best left in the hands of professional growers.

A base made of spiralling birch branches makes a natural setting for a living, potted cyclamen (from the garden or the florist). Begin with a suitable container for your plant—a margarine tub or other small plastic bowl. Then hot-glue and wire the container to the base so that it is positioned off-center near the bottom. After inserting your plant into the container, hot-glue pieces of sheet moss over the container to obscure it, and continue the moss onto the wreath base on either side of the plant. Insert some stems of dried sugarbush or other delicate white flower, and finish the arrangement with a colorful grosgrain ribbon lazily looped around the wreath. The ribbon can be secured with dots of hot glue where necessary. If properly cared for, your plant should bloom continuously for weeks or months.

Without a doubt, gladiolus is one of the most spectacular flowering plants. Their stalks can grow as tall as six feet (1.8 m) and are laden with flowers up to six inches (15 cm) wide. Gladioli bloom throughout the summer, and you can achieve a succession of blooms by staggering the planting. Most glads are tender, requiring the corms to be dug and stored through the winter.

Such an ostentatious flower as the gladiolus demands a base large enough to let it flaunt its glory. For this, grapevines are ideal, for they allow you to construct a base as large as you need. Hot-glue and wire a caged oasis holder at the bottom to provide moisture to the flowers. Then add six or seven stems of flowers, cutting them to uneven lengths. Using the height of the stems as a design element, create strong horizontal and vertical lines. To secure the tall stems, stretch and twist some floral tape, and use the resulting "vine" to attach them to the base. (See page 22 for guidance.) Add a few stems of sweet peas for texture, some bits of sheet moss to hide the oasis, and your wreath is complete.

53

Photograph by Tim Barnwell

ANNUALS

IF PERENNIALS ARE *the meat and potatoes of a garden, annuals are the ice cream sundaes. True, they last just one season, but oh, what a glorious scene! They quickly erupt into a profusion of bright tropical colors or the palest pastels, offering an endless array of combinations. Annuals are remarkably versatile; after just a few weeks of summer sun, they can fill an awkward gap, line a walkway, or scale a trellis. They come in all shapes and sizes and, unlike their hardier cousins, annuals will bloom for months on end. Many are fragrant, and most make excellent cut flowers. In fact, the more you cut them, the more they will bloom.*

Clearly the flowers of choice for the beginning gardener, annuals are inexpensive and offer plenty of opportunities to experiment. They are also your best bet if you want to try to grow plants from seed. When planting them from seeds, you must take into account that there are three types of annuals: hardy, half-hardy, and tender.

Hardy varieties such as larkspur and pansy are the most robust of annuals. Their seedlings can survive freezing weather, making it possible to plant seeds in the fall or in early spring as soon as the ground can be worked. Unfortunately, the flip side of their tolerance to cold is their incompatibility with heat. When the midsummer sun becomes a blast furnace, your hardy annuals are likely to wither.

Half-hardy annuals are the "middle-of-the-road" sort. The seeds should be sown in the spring only after the danger of frost has passed, else the delicate young plants will be nipped. Toward the end of the season, an established plant can easily survive a light fall frost. However, even a mature plant will succumb to a prolonged cold spell or a thorough freeze. Examples include the snapdragon, globe amaranth, and nasturtium.

As the name suggests, tender annuals are the most delicate. Don't let the imposing size of the sunflower or the rugged appearance of the cockscomb deceive you; a light frost can be deadly to these and other tender annuals. Their seeds can be planted only when the soil has warmed and there is no possibility of frost.

Although the annuals you plant will last just one season, you may be surprised by a new crop springing up the following year. This is because the plants frequently reseed themselves. The seeds themselves can survive freezing temperatures and, if left to their own devices, they are scattered by wind, rain, and birds. The result is that you may see new flowers sprout quite a distance from where you carefully placed the parent plant the year before. It is nature's way of adding serendipity to a gardener's plans.

THE ANNUAL FLOWER LARKSPUR (Consolida) *and the perennial delphinium are so similar in appearance that they are often confused and the names used interchangeably, even by professionals. Larkspur is somewhat daintier than delphinium, topping out at four feet (1.2 m) rather than six (1.8 m). When cut, its flowers are long lasting and dry easily.*

Here a profusion of larkspur is nestled into a wreath base made of blueberry twigs. You can purchase this type of base or make one of your own by wiring bunches of blueberry twigs about six inches (15 cm) long to a wire ring. Select the more graceful ends of the branches to fan outward, and arrange them in a spiral around the wreath form. Working from the center toward the outside, use a dab of hot glue to secure short spikes of larkspur in the same spiral pattern. At the top of the wreath, make a bow with wire-edged ribbon, and let the ends cascade in swirls down the sides. Hot-glue the ribbon in place.

THIS LOVELY GARDEN SCENE *recreates one of those fleet-ing moments of beauty to be found only in nature. Deep pur-ple, lavender, and rose blossoms spring forth from cool, green moss that makes an inviting resting spot for three feathered friends. A fourth swoops "overhead" in a cornhusk sky. The base for this wreath is a study in recycling. You can use any plump base—foam, straw, or vine—and it doesn't matter if* *it's shabby looking. Dampen the cornhusks to make them pliable, and attach them with white glue to the base. There is only one trick to creating this scene yourself: lay a wire across the wreath temporarily to support the tall flower stems as you attach them to the base with hot glue. Cover the ends of the stems with sheet moss, and place the birds with dabs of hot glue.*

MINIATURE PINCUSHIONS of color, globe amaranths (Gomphrena) are a versatile flower in the wreath maker's storehouse. The pink, purple, orange, and white globes resemble clover in their appearance, but they are stiff and prickly to the touch. The flower heads are made up of many rows of spiny bracts, not petals, and the tiny yellow spikes that appear between the layers are the actual flowers.

To make this delicate wreath, start with a base made of artificial greenery. Using a glue gun, attach three-inch (8 cm)

pieces of artemisia and German statice so that they fan out all around the outer edge of the base. Repeat around the inner ring. Then fill the top surface with a broad band of globe amaranth, interspersed here and there with miniature roses and pearly everlasting. With a fabric ribbon of complementing colors, tie a simple bow and glue it to the bottom of the wreath. In the center of the bow, attach a tiny nosegay made with a single rose bud, pearly everlasting, and a few sprigs of statice.

*L*IKE BERRIES RIPE *for the plucking, these deep magenta globes beckon the eye and the hand. They rest on a ring base that has been completely covered with German statice. Using a plastic or metal ring covered with floral tape, wire on short bunches of German statice all around. Overlap each bundle just enough to cover the stems of the preceding one. Place the amaranths together with small clusters of rue, white annual statice, and larkspur in shades of lavender and purple, hot-gluing them in place. Mountain mint leaves provide hints of greenery.*

ONE OF THE MOST POP-ULAR of the everlastings, strawflowers (Helichrysum) maintain their appearance extremely well when dried. In fact, you almost have to touch the blossoms to deter-mine whether they are fresh or dried. When fully open, the flower's central disc is surrounded by several layers of stiff bracts that resemble petals. If you prefer them partially unopened, with some of the bracts still closed over the center, pick the flowers when their outer lay-ers are just starting to spread. They will continue to open somewhat after cutting.

This flower-filled wreath begins with an artificial ever-green base. To provide a flo-ral background, German statice is hot-glued around the base in a circular pat-tern. Strawflowers at various stages of blooming are then glued onto the wreath, together with accents of globe amaranth, celosia, miniature roses, pearly everlasting, and nigella pods. As a final touch, a satin ribbon bow is attached at the bottom.

A FAVORITE WITH CHILDREN *and adults, sunflowers (Helianthus) quickly grow to giant proportions, looming over the rest of the garden. And, as anyone who regularly feeds birds knows, they readily sprout from seeds. Some, like the blossoms used to make this cheerful wreath, are much more modest in scale. To make the wreath, begin by wiring short clusters of German statice onto a plastic or metal ring covered with floral tape. German statice is very brittle and can be prickly to handle. Misting it with water and leaving it overnight makes the material much easier to manipulate. With the base complete, hot-glue the miniature sunflowers into prominent positions all around the wreath. To get a three-dimensional appearance, try to glue the flowers deep inside and outside the wreath, not just on the top. Add clusters of chinaberries, white annual statice, and stems of wheat.*

*E*QUALLY WELL KNOWN *by its horticultural name—Celosia—and its common name—cockscomb—this plant is an old-fashioned favorite for cutting and drying. The crested variety closely resembles brilliantly colored ocean coral formations with its dense, convoluted ridges. The taller, plumed variety is dramatic in the garden and in dried arrangements, but is less commonly used in wreath making.*

When dried, cockscomb flowers are soft and furry to the touch. Massed together, as they are in this elegant wreath, they beckon you to bury your face in their velvety richness.

Here, tight knots of the deepest, darkest red are complemented by frilly ruffles of bright scarlet, producing a subtle drama that has no need for any further embellishment. To make this wreath, start with a double wire ring, and cover it with Spanish moss to make a rounded form. Then wrap a dark red velvet ribbon around the base. The ribbon hides any small gaps that may occur between the blossoms. Hot-glue the flower heads in place, varying the height and angle to give the wreath fullness and depth.

AN ALTERNATIVE APPROACH *is to use light, airy silver king artemisia as a perfect contrast for the cockscomb's
dense mounds. Half a dozen sweetheart roses and clusters of
pepperberries echo the soft magenta theme, while neon-bright
miniature bouquets of statice are strategically placed for visual
excitement. Begin by wrapping scrap pieces of artemisia
around a single wire ring, building the circle to a thickness of*
*about 3/4 inch (2 cm), and securing them around the ring
with monofilament (fishing line). Take small bunches of silver
king artemisia, each about four inches (10 cm) long, and
anchor them to the base with monofilament or wire. Using a
glue gun, secure the cockscomb evenly around the top, and
place the roses, berries, and statice where your eye tells you
they belong.*

Young and old alike delight in the fanciful nature of snapdragons (Antirrhinum), from their ruffled skirts to their obliging habit of popping their mouths open whenever their blossoms are squeezed. They're easily grown from seed in sizes ranging from dwarf (6 inches/15 cm) to giant (as tall as three feet/one meter) and in nearly every color.

This assortment represents a full garden of color. Individual stems are cut to varying lengths and inserted into a thoroughly dampened oasis base, completely covering the wreath with blossoms. Arrange the colors to suit your taste, reserving the brightest ones for prominant highlights. For an extra embellishment, loop a narrow satin ribbon among the blooms, securing the ribbon at several locations with floral picks.

*T*HESE CREAMY YELLOW *snaps stand tall and proud amidst a lush wreath covered with shiny box-wood. They are accompanied by tiny montecasino asters, a clutch of variegated pittospo-rum, and a few rakish whips of curly willow. In lieu of a ready-made base, this wreath utilizes a wire frame filled with floral oasis which, if soaked before-hand and periodi-cally misted, will keep the flowers and greenery fresh for several days. Simply insert the stems, each cut on an angle, directly into the soft oasis.*

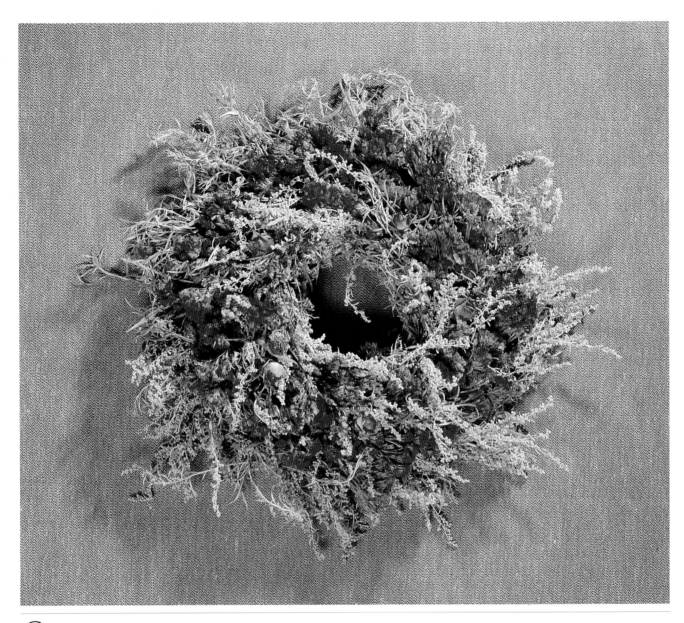

ONE OF THE BEST *flowers for drying, statice
(Limonium) has its home near beaches and sea marshes.
Many of the most popular colors issue from the
Mediterranean region. Surprisingly sturdy, the plant can with-
stand both periodic salt spray and ocean storms. It is an
equally durable everlasting, and numerous hybrids have been
developed to increase the color range of the native plants.*

*Dried statice in deep, royal purple is combined with cotton-
candy pink statice, cockscomb, and rose buds to make a
wreath that is almost good enough to eat. To create one of*
*your own, start with a base of Spanish moss. Form small
bunches of artemisia, and pin them in a spiral around the
inside and outside edges of the base. After thoroughly misting
the statice with water, pin small bundles of the purple flowers
around the outer rim of the wreath just inside the artemisia.
Next, make small bouquets of pink statice framed by
artemisia, and pin these into the uncovered spaces. Finally,
glue five tiny heads of pink cockscomb and five pink roses
around the wreath as accents.*

PEACH AND WHITE annual statice make a delightful spring-time combination. Start with a base made of German statice, and hot-glue clusters of each color of the native plant in random locations all around the base. Leave spaces between the clusters to fill with peach strawflowers and pink globe amaranths. Add accents of blackberry seed pods and stems of marjoram. For a greater sense of depth and color contrast, insert bay leaves intermittently around the outside and inner ring of the wreath, adding just a few in the center as well.

A WELCOME ALTERNATIVE to overly common impatiens, the begonia is one of the few flowering plants that flourishes in full shade. Begonias come in two types: the wax begonia with dainty single or double flowers and bright, glistening foliage; and the more lavish tuberous begonia whose flowers have layer upon layer of petals. Both types produce an abundance of flowers throughout the summer, and the tuberous varieties can be dug up and saved over the winter to be replanted the next spring.

Fire-engine red petals and deep, dark leaves mark this wreath made of wax begonias. It couldn't be simpler to construct; just cut individual stems of flowers and foliage, and insert them at various angles into a well-soaked oasis base.

TINY WHITE AMMOBIUM blossoms—also called winged everlasting—look like twinkling stars in this dramatic wreath of feathery preserved ferns. To make this quick and easy base, attach bundles of the preserved fern to a wire ring. (The designer used a Hillman Handi-Ring, a single metal ring with built-in clips for holding the materials in place.) Prepare several bunches of ammobium, each with multiple stems of varying length, and tape the ends for easy insertion into the wreath base. Cut ten dried roses with short stems, ten sprigs of larkspur about 6 inches (15 cm) long, and ten santolina flower tops. Carefully hot-glue the ammobium bunches evenly around the base, with the flower ends pointed out and slightly upward. At the base of each bunch of ammobium, glue a rose, a sprig of larkspur, and a yellow button-top of santolina. Fill in the wreath with additional short, single stems of ammobium as needed for additional pinpoints of light.

PANSIES (VIOLA) *are among the first annual plants to be set out in the garden because they can easily with-stand a night's frost. Ranging in color from pure white to a deep, dark purple that looks almost black, pansies are ver-satile, easy-to-grow plants that fit into any landscape.*

Here clusters of pansies in several colors mass together for a full, sumptuous wreath. Begin with a well-moistened oasis base, either purchased or constructed (see page 20 for details). Cut a basketful of pansies, and cluster them into small bunches. To make it easier to insert the delicate stems into the oasis, fasten each bouquet to a floral pick. Then insert the picked clusters all around the wreath base, packing the flowers together for complete coverage.

L OVE-IN-A-MIST (Nigella) *is probably more commonly recognized by its papery seed pods, which are prized by wreath makers and floral designers alike. With their broad burgundy stripes against a pale green background, the pods make dramatic accents in all manner of floral arrangements. Not to be neglected, the flowers closely resemble bachelor's buttons but with longer tendrils on each petallike bract. It makes a good cut flower but tends to wilt when dried.*

Lavender-blue and pink blossoms, some cut short and others left longer, grace an elegantly simple, country-style wreath made of raffia. To construct the base, simply take a clump of raffia, and tie it into a knot at the top. Using a few extra strands of raffia, clasp the base together at several points. Then clip off any loose ends at the knots. Wire a well-soaked bouquet holder onto the bottom of the base, and insert the flowers along with a few galax leaves and stems of variegated ivy. Use bits of Spanish moss to hide any of the mechanics.

BROAD, DAISYLIKE BLOSSOMS *and rounded doubles characterize zinnias, which bloom in a rainbow of colors. As cut flowers they often last for weeks, and when dried in silica gel, zinnias lose none of their vibrant color and maintain their full petal size and shape.*

To make this bright, midsummer wreath, start with a wire ring base. Enlarge the base and give it some resilience by wrapping scrap pieces of artemisia all around, securing them in place with monofilament. Then make small bundles of four-inch (10 cm) pieces of artemisia, and attach these around the base in a uniform spiral. Tuck in pieces of lavender-grey caspia, and top the wreath with zinnias and pieces of purple larkspur. To prevent the fragile petals of the zinnias from breaking off, attach the flowers with a ring of hot glue dotted onto the backs of the petals. A navy satin bow adds the finishing touch.

ROSE EVERLASTING (Helichrysum), *so called for its excellence in drying, is a delicate, daisylike flower that has stiff, papery bracts surrounding a circle of tiny florets. Its sturdy stem assures that this flower will not droop or break, even after thorough drying.*

In this wreath, an everyday vine base is transformed into a miniature garden scene with the addition of a rustic-looking wooden fence, a pole-mounted birdhouse, and a pair of artifi-

cial birds. The fence can be made from thick sections of grapevine (to match the wreath) or from twigs. With brown yarn, tie the fence onto the back of the wreath base; then hotglue the birdhouse in place. Thoroughly mist some sheet moss, and glue it onto the wreath below the fence. Attach rose everlastings along the bottom of the fence to form a garden, placing a few so that they peek out between the posts. Finally, perch a couple of tiny birds in comfortable-looking positions.

THE BOTANICAL NAME of this flower, Xeranthemum, *derives from the Greek for "dry flower." It is indicative of* the papery texture of its dainty double flowers, which grow in a wide variety of colors. Its common name, immortelle, is equally fitting for a flower that dries so successfully.

Because of its diminutive size, immortelle is better suited to a small scale wreath. Start with a ring base evenly covered with miniature bouquets of German statice. The statice makes an attractive background in the spaces between your more significant flowers. To add the immortelle blossoms, touch each stem with a drop of hot glue, and insert it into the base. For a bit of contrast, add a few stems of dark blue larkspur and some individual mountain mint leaves in key locations around the wreath. For embellishment, attach a casual bow of fine satin ribbon.

WILDFLOWERS

EVERY SPECIES OF FLOWER *was once a wildflower, found only where nature placed it. Gradually, as their culinary, medicinal, or mystical value was recognized by various cultures, many flowers were first cultivated and later hybridized to produce more desirable plants. Travelers brought back seeds and small plants from faraway places, and soon the foreign plants were thoroughly intermingled with the native ones.*

By the time flowers were recognized simply for their beauty, mankind was already flexing its muscle to shape the form, color, and growth habits of the more popular ones. Controlled cross-pollination and extensive breeding programs have resulted in flowers that are ever larger, more colorful, or otherwise more desirable to the public. Nevertheless, despite our efforts to "civilize" our environment, some flowers continue to be relative renegades.

Why should we be interested in these more modest natives when there are all sorts of glamorous exotic plants available? The answer is threefold. First, to find flowers growing in the woods, along a stream bed, or scattered across a field is to experience the magic and mystery of nature. It is humbling to witness the simple beauty of flowers blooming merely to reproduce themselves, not to fit within a design contrived by human intellect.

Second, to plant native flowers in your immediate surroundings is to recreate the landscape that was there before you were born. With the influx of more roads and more housing developments, much of the original vegetation has been destroyed or, at the least, altered. On a limited scale you can restore that which has vanished— an open prairie, a rock-filled mountain stream, or a bit of the desert.

Third, and probably most convincing, it is usually easier to grow native plants than to cultivate exotic varieties. After all, they're the flowers best adapted to your conditions—frequent summer downpours, heavy clay soil, and the like. Many people have taken up the idea of planting wildflowers mainly to rid themselves of the unceasing demands of a lawn.

From the standpoint of making floral wreaths, wildflowers are often more subtle than their exotic counterparts. Their smaller size and more delicate form draw in the viewer, and their lack of flamboyance fits well within the simpler lifestyle many are trying to accomplish.

Unfortunately, as interest has grown in using wildflowers in the garden, there has been a corresponding depletion of native plants in the wild. Although most are easily propagated in backyard gardens, a huge majority of native plants being sold has been collected from the wild. If you're interested in growing wildflowers for enjoyment and making wreaths, please try to obtain them from suppliers who propagate rather than dig their stock.

ONCE COMMON EUROPEAN *wildflowers, yarrows (Achillea) have found their way into the hearts—and gardens—of many flower lovers. It's not difficult to understand why. These easily grown perennials have massive, colorful blossoms and aromatic, fernlike foliage. They are long lasting when cut, and they dry well, maintaining much of their distinctive color.*

The rich, amber tones of this arrangement are testimony to yarrow's staying power when dried. To make this wreath *yourself, simply clip the heads off about 40 to 50 dried yarrow blossoms. Apply hot glue, and attach them to a vine base. For an informal, less structured look, apply the flowers haphazardly rather than in a spiral. When you have an arrangement you like, add a simple bow made with a few strands of raffia. Glue the bow into one of the flower heads, and arrange the loose raffia tendrils around the base. To complete the composition, position two artificial birds onto the wreath as if they are pausing to rest during their migratory flight.*

CREAMY WHITE YARROW *adorns this springlike wreath made of twisted vines that have been overlaid across the bottom to suggest the form of a basket. Bundles of lamb's ears are hot-glued across the back, forming a pearly green background for the flowers. Intermingled with the yarrow are peach-colored strawflowers and a few single lamb's ears. Along the front rim of the basket, a snatch of lace adds a dainty touch. A bow made of narrow peach ribbon rests jauntily on one side.*

A EUROPEAN NATIVE, *bachelor's buttons* (Centaurea cyanus) *have naturalized freely throughout North America. Also called cornflowers, these bright blue flowers are commonly found along country roads to greet motorists and hikers during the early summer.*

Echoing the plant's wild nature, this wreath is built upon a grapevine base that has sprigs of contorted filbert tucked into several locations. To provide moisture to the flowers, hot-glue a small caged oasis to the base, covering it with bits of sheet moss. Then place the bachelor's buttons and their grasslike buds into the oasis in a strong, linear design. If you keep the oasis moist and the flowers misted, this wreath will easily keep its freshness for several days.

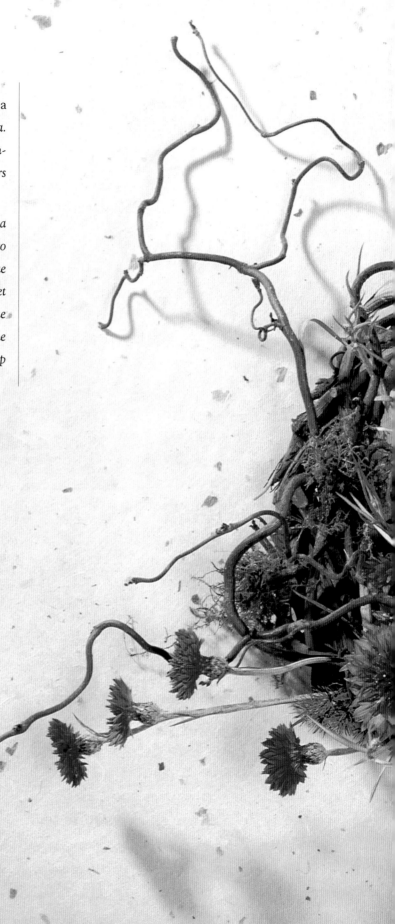

LONG TUBULAR FLOWERS *in white and shades of pink and purple characterize beard-tongue (Penstemon). This lovely plant received its rather unfortunate common name due to the fact that one of its stamens is large and flat, resembling a tongue, and it is frequently bearded. Given its many pluses, this plant is vastly underutilized. The flowers are naturally attractive to hummingbirds, and they are long-lasting when cut. A midsummer bloomer, it will hold its green leaves until well after the first frost.*

Beard-tongue makes a full, yet dainty wreath, especially when complemented with other delicate flowers and foliage. Begin with a moist oasis wreath form, and insert short pieces of fennel interspersed with stems of artemisia. When the colors are evenly distributed, add enough beard-tongue to fill the wreath with pink color. Finally, accent the wreath with short lengths of lady's-mantle for a bit of coarser texture.

SALVIA, ALSO COM-
MONLY *called sage, is one of*
several plants whose various
species include both annuals
and perennials. Blue salvia,
or mealycup sage (Salvia
farinacea), is considered a
tender perennial. In its native
Texas and New Mexico, it
thrives in lime-rich soils on
hillsides and in prairies, thick-
ets, and meadows. Blue
salvia's small, delicate flowers
are beloved by bees. When
dried, it is an excellent mater-
ial for making wreaths.

A finely textured wreath
results when you pair blue
salvia with German statice.
Begin with a wire ring base,
and wrap bunches of the sta-
tice onto the ring with mono-
filament. Starting at the top,
attach the bunches down
both sides until they meet in
the middle at the bottom.
Using hot glue, attach small
clusters of salvia to the bot-
tom two-thirds of the wreath,
making a crescent shape.
Finish with a white bow and
a single pink rose.

EACH TINY BOUQUET *in the broad, flat head of a*
Queen Anne's lace (Daucus) blossom is made up of numer-
ous minuscule florets. This flower's intricacy easily lives up to
its common name. A member of the carrot family, the plant
has a root that resembles the familiar vegetable, but it is not
edible.

For so delicate-looking a flower, Queen Anne's lace dries
remarkably well. When dried, its wide umbrella heads become
a mellow gold, about the color of hay. Here several large,
well-formed flower tops of Queen Anne's lace mingle grace-
fully with deep, dark red roses and spikes of Mexican sage.
All are hot-glued onto a grapevine base. To frame the compo-
sition, fern tips and rose leaves are inserted along the inner
and outer edges of the wreath.

A CULTIVATED VARIETY *of this beloved wildflower has less distinct floral crowns. Long, delicate stems separate the individual clusters of tiny florets and, in a bunch, it is difficult to distinguish where one flower ends and another begins. They're perfect for an untamed wreath bursting with midsummer energy. The base is made from dried grasses twisted and wired together. Any visible wire is hidden with bits of moss. A bouquet holder provides moisture to a half-dozen stems of Queen Anne's lace and several golden asters, which are arranged in an overall triangular pattern to accent the Queen Anne's lace. Leatherleaf fern covers the miniature oasis, and a bright yellow bow accents the flowers.*

THE PITCHER PLANT (Sarracenia) *is one of nature's most interesting woodland plants. The name is reflective of the plant's upright posture and its enlarged opening that is always partially full of water. Insects that fall into the pitcher have trouble escaping the pool of water because small downward-facing hairs line the inside surface of the flower. The dissolved proteins from the victims help feed the plant. Due to their relative scarcity in the wild, don't pick any pitcher plants you may find in the woods. Instead, order them from commercial growers who provide the flowers already dried.*

The quiet color and dramatic shape of the pitcher plant make it an important component of this glorious wreath. Preserved oak leaves, stems of bittersweet, and bunches of bay leaves are applied to a large vine base to set the stage for the flowers. First the dried pitcher plants, then mahogany pods, are arranged in a radiating pattern up from the bottom center. The sides are filled in with strawflowers, globe amaranth and thistle, nigella, clusters of pepperberries, and clumps of yarrow and Browneii hyacinth. Three artichokes are wired, then glued together with two pitcher plants, and the cluster is inserted at the top center. A bow of French ribbon crowns the artichoke grouping, and long streamers drape artistically down each side. For dramatic effect, two additional lengths of ribbon are looped around twigs and inserted in either side.

Many gardeners abhor thistles (Cirsium), no less for their invasive habits than for their thorny stems, leaves, and flowers. The rich, purple blooms are handsome, though, and make a dramatic addition to the wreath maker's palette. Some of the cultivated varieties have less prickly stems and leaves yet retain the characteristic spiny heads of wild thistles.

A heart-shaped wreath covered with cornhusks is evocative of the open pastures where wild thistles can often be found growing. To make this simple, country arrangement, hot-glue dried bay leaves around the top surface of the wreath form. Cut several flower tops from a bouquet of dried thistles, and glue them between the bay leaves, about 1-1/2 inches (4 cm) apart, leaving room at the center top for a bow. Between the flower tops, fill in with short-stemmed thistles, arranging the stemmed flowers to show the sides of the blossoms. For a final accent, make a bow of narrow ribbon, and glue it to the center top. You can hide the wire used to make the bow by gluing one or two thistle blossoms over it.

JOE-PYE WEED (Eupatorium) *is a North American native whose domed flower clusters can reach up to four inches (10 cm) across. Legend says the plant takes its name from a New England tribal medicine man who used it to cure typhus. However, the tribal word for typhus, jopi, is a likelier source. If you plan to dry the flowers, collect them just as they begin to bloom (August or September); otherwise, the dried blossoms may become too brittle to handle.*

To construct this luxurious wreath, begin by assembling flower clusters onto picks. The best approach is to separate the individual flower heads, and group several together. Altogether, about 40 or 50 clusters are needed. Cover the inner and outer edges of the wreath form; then fill in the top surface, leaving space along one side for the accent materials. Make small bundles of artemisia and statice, picking them into the wreath in a crescent shape. Combine lace and moiré ribbons to form a three- or five-loop bow with long streamers. After securing the loops with wire, pick the bow into the base. Then attach a few dried roses and some additional accent flowers on either side of the bow. Finally, curl and loop the ribbon streamers, and hold them in place with a few dabs of hot glue.

BLACK-EYED SUSAN (Rudbeckia) *is one of the most prevalent of "roadside weeds." Depending on local conditions, this plant can be an annual, biennial, or a short-lived perennial. As a biennial, the young plants develop in late summer, overwinter, and bloom the following season. The "eye" of the blossom is actually a collection of minute, dark purple, disk-shaped flowers.*

Resembling a Roman crown of glory, this golden crescent has at its center a clutch of dried black-eyed Susan blossoms. The

flower's large, dark eyes remain undiminished by the drying process, and the amber petals curl to a striking halo. On either side of the black-eyed Susans sit towering spikes of loosestrife and purple columns of anise hyssop. These, together with dried marigolds, ox-eyed daisies, dusty miller, and cork leaves, curve up along both sides of the wreath. Each flower is tucked into the twisting vine base and secured there with a bit of hot glue.

*H*ILLSIDES AND SUN-
DRENCHED *fields are com-
mon homes for the purple
coneflower (Echinacea). It
blooms in late summer, frequently lasting into fall. Unlike
most daisylike blossoms, the
lavender petals of these flowers
curve downward, forming a
skirt below the prominent con-
ical center. When dried, the
petals tend to curl, but neither
they nor the spiny center lose
their rich purple color.*

*A wildflower wreath deserves
a suitable base, and this one is
formed from stems of fresh
mugwort, an herb. Alternatively, a small vine wreath
would work very nicely. Press
small bunches of baby's-breath
around the bottom three-
quarters of the wreath, hot-
gluing them in place if necessary. (This wreath uses a combination of wild and cultivated
baby's-breath for textural
diversity.) On either side, add
clusters of fountain grass, oats,
and a few purple coneflowers.
Reserve most of the coneflowers for the top and bottom,
where they are attached with
hot glue. Fill in any gaps with
stems of red yarrow to complete the natural look.*

A BELOVED FLOWER *found in fields and meadows*
everywhere, buttercups (Ranunculus) have such glossy flowers that you might think they're perpetually wet. When paired
with other natives of the fields—crimson clover and bachelor's buttons—they make a delightful wreath. These wildflowers have slender stems, and you will have greater success

making a wreath if you use spring oasis (a softer form of
floral oasis that is made to hold delicate stems) fastened into a
wire ring. After dousing the oasis with water, insert your
background materials: several sprigs of artemisia and a few
leaves of evening primrose. Then add scads of buttercups and
a sprinkling of clover and bachelor's buttons.

CHINESE-LANTERNS (Physalis), *also called ground-cherries, are members of the nightshade family. This group of plants also includes tomatoes, peppers, and petunias. The genus name means bladder, a fitting reference to the papery pods that contain the plant's seeds.*

For a less conventional approach to a wreath, allow the typical doughnut-shaped profile to flatten into a woven heart made of grapevine. When decorated with a spray of Chinese-lanterns, it becomes a handsome autumnal display. The base of the spray is a length of wide, plaid fabric ribbon curved diagonally across the heart frame. To make a graceful curve, twist and wire the center of the ribbon to a point in the upper

left portion of the wreath base. Forming a gentle curve, glue the ends of the ribbon to the edges of the wreath. Make two similar bouquets, each consisting of a few stems of sweet Annie, a bundle of santolina flowers, a stem containing several Chinese-lanterns, and a few sprigs of baby's-breath. Before securing them with floral tape, add a delicate birch branch to each bouquet. Place the bouquets on top of the ribbon, facing the ends outward. Then wire them in place, and cover the connection with a bow made of the same plaid ribbon.

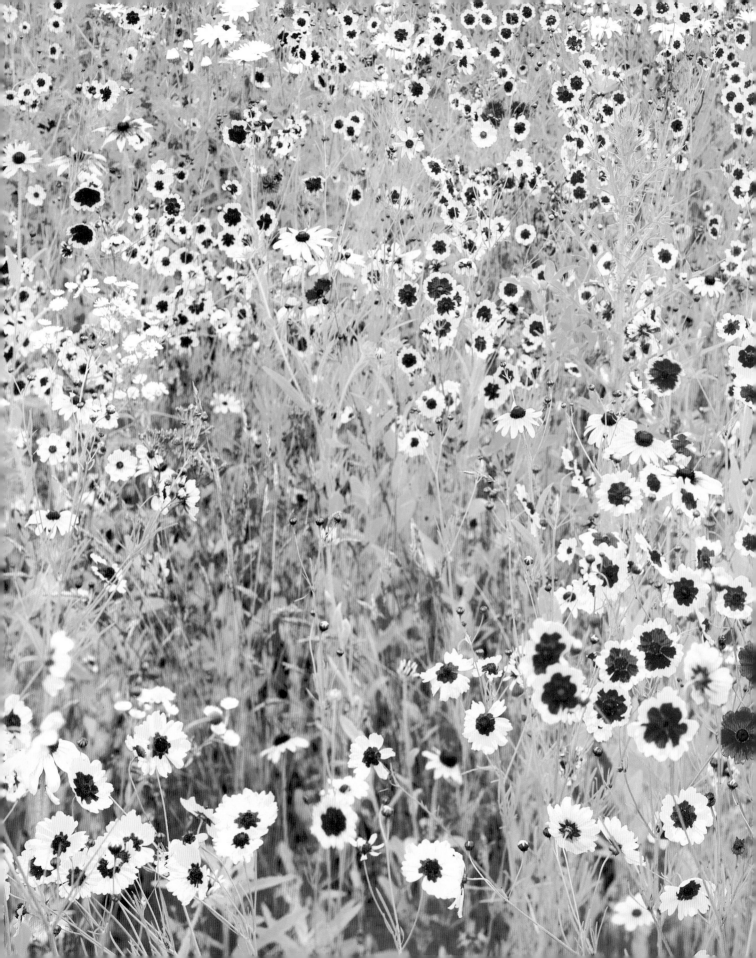

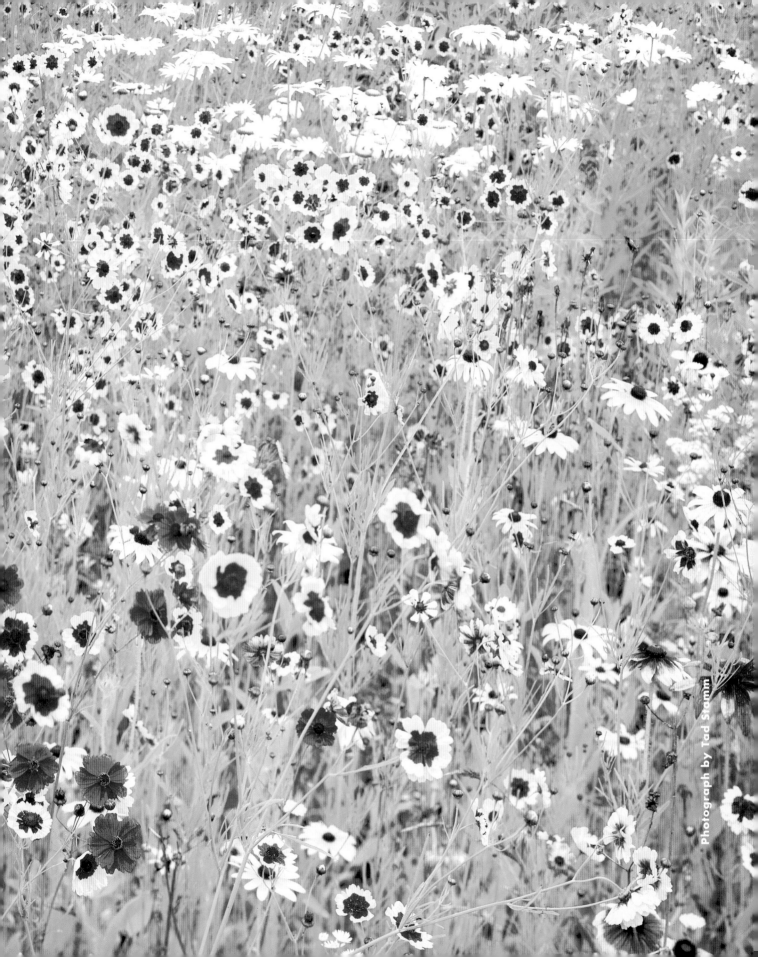

Photograph by Tad Stamm

FLOWERING SHRUBS

IF YOU LOVE FLOWERS, *there's no way to get more bang for your buck than by planting flowering shrubs. Where flowering plants provide bright touches, a single shrub can easily produce masses of color. In a landscape otherwise filled with junipers and boxwoods, a flowering shrub brings relief; in a flower-filled garden, it adds scale and dimension.*

The major advantage to flowering shrubs is that they'll last your lifetime or well beyond it. Antique roses that bloom season after season around the remains of a tumble-down country house attest to the staying power of shrubs. If you invest the time and energy into setting them into the ground properly, and they have sufficient amounts of sunlight, water, and nutrients, flowering shrubs are remarkably reliable.

They're also relatively worry-free. In terms of their care, shrubs are quite a contrast to annuals that must be put out new each season, bulbs that need dividing, and perennials that require all manner of attention to assure good growth patterns. Once you've placed a shrub, it's there. There is no need to dig it up, divide the roots, and resettle it into a newly fertilized bed.

To those tackling a new garden area, planting some flowering shrubs is one of the first steps you can and should take to shape your space. Shrubs are like a skeleton: they provide the framework for all of the smaller elements that fill in around them.

With respect to color, form, and fragrance, the flowers from shrubs have everything to offer that other flowers do, except that there are a lot more of them. A single lilac bush can produce more blossoms than you can imagine cutting; their perfume would be overpowering in the house. Unlike a herbaceous plant, where cutting several blooms may produce quite a gap, you will hardly notice the same loss from a shrub.

In addition to their flowers, many shrubs develop berries that attract birds and other wildlife to your garden. Most are also deciduous, and their leaves turn brilliant colors in autumn. After the leaves drop, the branches of the shrub remain as a sculptural addition to the winter landscape.

No matter what your constraints, there are shrubs that will accommodate them. Whether your area is open and sun-drenched or shaded by tall trees, numerous shrubs will oblige by blooming there. Neither are you limited by growth habit. They come in dwarf sizes as well as giant varieties. Some are tall and slender, others short and wide. In short, when it comes to flowering shrubs, there is truly something for everyone.

WITCH HAZEL (Hamamelis) *is a favorite shrub for gardeners because it is one of the few that bloom in the winter. With their snaky tendrils, the blossoms look like miniature Medusas. Its unusual common name derives from the fact that the shrub's branches were often used to dowse for water, a process also known as "water witching." As the flowers dry, the petals tend to shrivel a bit, but they keep their color.*

As displayed by this feathery wreath, witch hazel blooms in shades of yellow and red. Several short stems are wired onto a small straw base that has been covered with furry geum leaves. For some added color, a few branches of early-blooming spirea and honeysuckle are kept fresh in a floral tube wired to the wreath base. The tube is hidden by a clutch of heather, and the wreath is further enhanced by a few sprigs of lavender and black pussy willow stems.

R OSES (Rosa) *are by far the most popular flowering shrub throughout the world. They have been grown by every ancient civilization from China to the Mediterranean. Throughout the years as styles have evolved, roses have been hybridized to meet new tastes. Still they reign supreme as the king of flowers.*

The untamed look of a wreath made of bear grass provides an interesting counterpoint to these refined "Sonya" roses. To construct this unusual base, divide the bear grass (or any suitable long grass) into three or four bunches, securing the bottom of each bunch with wire, string, or rubber bands. Loop the grass into a wreath shape, adding one bunch at a time, and gluing or wiring the bunches together. Be sure to leave some ends trailing freely. For a less vibrant color, the wreath can be set aside for several days in a hot, dry area, where it will fade to a pale, dusty green. To attach the flowers, wire a well-soaked oasis holder onto the base. Then arrange the roses in a loose triangle with the larger blooms nearer the foam and the smaller ones at the points of the triangle. Tuck bits of moss and extra rose foliage around the roses to camouflage the stems and holder.

101

MOST ROSES ARE DRIED *while still in bud, but these have been allowed to open to their full opulence. In this scene, they are about to become part of a luxurious home for two bluebirds. To create the setting for this colorful activity, begin with a vine base covered with moss or lichens. Before attaching it to the base, mist the moss with water and trim off any bits of dirt and bark. Concentrating the floral adornment in a single quarter of the wreath, start with an oval of rose leaves. Using hot glue, attach three large roses, two dried jonquils, and a few stems of delphinium. Position a small rosebud near each full rose blossom, and fill any holes with larkspur and tips of baby's-breath. As a final step, glue the birds in place, fixing a narrow ribbon between their beaks.*

*T*HESE PALE PEACH *"Oshiana" roses, the color of cool alabaster, are glorious in their dewy freshness. The blossoms are cut at various stages of opening and are inserted directly into an oasis base. Glistening, deep burgundy-green galax leaves and feathery soft ming fern surround the blooms.*

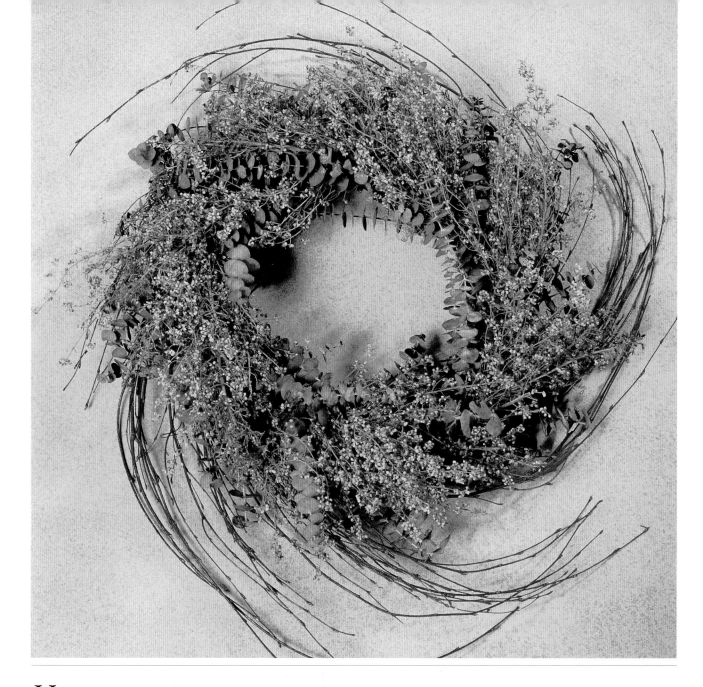

HEATHERS (Calluna *and* Erica) *are low-growing shrubs that can be found blanketing the ground throughout the British Isles where they are native. Heathers and their close relatives, heaths, are often planted in a mixture of varieties to obtain a tapestry of color and texture. In folklore, heather brings good fortune and health. A family that has heather growing will have happiness.*

Representing two extremes of climate, the combination of fresh heather with eucalyptus may seem an unlikely marriage. The results, however, are both gorgeous and fragrant. The curving branches of the birch base establish a powerful sense of motion that is reinforced by the spiralling arrangement of flowers and foliage. Small bunches of eucalyptus combined with three or four stems of heather are each tied to the base with yarn to secure them. (You can use fine tweezers to thread the yarn between and around the branches of the base.) The application of each new bundle hides the attachment point of its predecessor, with the final bunch tucked under the first.

W ITH ITS LONG, arching branches of sunny yellow blossoms, forsythia is a welcome sight on a still frosty morning. It is one of the first shrubs to bloom in the waning weeks of winter and is easily forced if cut and brought into a warm room for a few days.

To make this exuberant wreath, first build a base from an old cinnamon broom. Use about half the broom, pulling the longer ends up and around to form a wreath shape. This cinnamon broom was sprayed with a burgundy paint, but you may prefer the natural color. After securing the wreath at top and bottom, attach a small bouquet holder at the bottom center. Insert a few long stems of forsythia into the bouquet holder, bend them around to form large loops, and tuck or wire them in place. Add some shorter stems of forsythia on either side, and place a plaid bow in the center. Use a few sprigs of boxwood to cover the mechanics and three alstroemeria blossoms and bits of leptospermum for contrasting color.

A STAPLE IN HOME GARDENS *for generations, the common lilac (Syringa) continues to spread its splendid blooms across the landscape today. The original species plants are limited to the familiar lavender and white single flowers, but numerous hybrids have been developed with larger, fluffier blossoms in colors ranging from yellow to burgundy-red. All have attractive foliage that makes a handsome windbreak or hedge.*

A wreath of French lilacs can easily fill a room with its romantic scent, and it offers a striking alternative to a conventional centerpiece for that special dinner party. Lilacs are fleeting, however; don't expect them to last more than a day or two once they're cut. To make this wreath, fill an oasis ring with three varieties of foliage: boxwood, pittosporum, and leatherleaf fern. Then insert stems of lilac blossoms (with a few leaves still attached) at random locations and angles around the ring.

107

RHODENDRONS AND AZALEAS all belong to the same genus, Rhododendron, and the flower forms of both are quite similar. Azaleas are the more petite of the two, and they can be found in both deciduous and evergreen varieties that grow in conditions ranging from full sun to open shade. Rhododendrons are generally shade-loving evergreens that can grow to towering sizes. In their native habitat, rhododendrons attain a height and trunk diameter equivalent to that of a small tree.

Because of the magnificence of their blossoms, as few as a half-dozen stems of rhododendron are sufficient to make a stunning wreath. Cut each stem with a sharp, angular cut, and leave enough of the stem so that the flower isn't flattened but shows its entire fullness. Then insert each one into a well-soaked oasis base.

*F*OR A MULTI-COLORED *array, select several different types of azalea for your wreath. Cut some flowers from each, and cluster them together into small bouquets. To make handling easier, wire the bouquets onto floral picks before insert-* *ing them into a moist oasis ring. Create the abundance of color you see here by placing the flower clusters close together and covering every available angle of the oasis base.*

FOR THOSE WHO HAVE *a shady site, there are relative-ly few options when it comes to flowering shrubs. One of the finest is the hydrangea. This shrub not only tolerates low light but actually prefers it, and even a young plant will produce a generous number of enormous flower clusters. Its nonwhite varieties exhibit an unusual sensitivity to soil conditions: in a sweet soil, the blossoms are pink; blue flowers result from an acidic soil.*

As evidenced by this lush wreath, hydrangea maintains all of its glory when dried. After drying, cut small clusters of the flowers, and assemble them onto picks. Begin on the inside circle of a straw wreath form, and pick the flowers on an angle into the base. Make a second circle of flower clusters around the outside of the wreath. Then, using a zigzag pattern, fill in the top surface, angling and layering the clusters to fill out the wreath. Add an accent ribbon by securing one cut end onto a pick, inserting it into the base, and looping and twining the ribbon as you desire. Finally, insert a small cluster of statice for a garnish.

BLUE FLOWERS ARE *uncommon in nature—most have a distinct lavender cast—and the quest for a true blue has inspired plant breeders and home gardeners for generations. Hydrangeas grown in an acid soil provide some of the bluest. In this wreath, the dried blossoms are arranged in a full circle on a* *generous bed of lemon leaves. Start with a crimped wire wreath frame, and wire the leaves in an even pattern around the circle. In the center of the leaves, hot-glue clumps of hydrangea evenly around. Finish with a bow of grosgrain ribbon.*

In EARLY TO MIDSPRING, *dwarf flowering almond* (Prunus glandulosa) *is blanketed with diminutive pink or white pompoms. As its botanical name indicates, the flowering almond is a member of the same genus as the cherry. Unlike the cherry, it produces no fruit. Its smaller scale—only about four feet (1.2 m) in height—makes it an ideal accent shrub for home landscaping.*

In this casual wreath, several branches of pink flowering almond blossoms form a generous corona at the top. They are poked into an oasis ring that has been covered with Spanish moss. Secure the moss with floral pins; they are easily hidden by the tendrils of the moss. To carry the pink theme throughout the wreath, casually loop and hot-glue a narrow satin ribbon to the moss in several places.

Slim, arching stems form a cascade of white, pink, or rosy red blossoms on spirea (Spiraea). Some varieties bloom in early spring, shortly after forsythia, while others wait until mid- or late summer to flower. The flowers grow in clusters that differ in size according to the variety; some, such as "bumalda" spirea, have gently domed clusters up to six inches (15 cm) across.

Known as "bridal veil," this variety of spirea has especially delicate flower clusters that blanket its branches. What the flowers lack in fragrance, they more than make up for in beauty; each blossom is like a miniature, fully opened rose. The fine stems are easily snapped and inserted into an oasis base. Vary the angle to ensure fullness and total coverage from every perspective. A few strands of wired pearls, picked into the wreath off-center at the top, add elegance to the white-on-white composition.

TROPICAL FLOWERS

UNLESS YOU LIVE IN A *tropical climate, there is an entire group of plants that just won't thrive in your backyard garden. Plants native to temperate climates have adapted to the yearly onslaught of winter weather, usually by receding into dormancy or by setting seed that is unaffected by frost. Those born in the tropics rely upon a steady combination of sunlight, warmth, and moisture.*

Human nature being what it is, there is a consistent demand for flowers that we desire merely because we don't see them in the landscape all around us. To satisfy that demand, commercial greenhouses have been established to grow tropical flowers, and many exotic blooms are flown in from all corners of the globe for distribution to local florists. As a result, in the midst of a cold, New England winter you can now make a wreath using flowers that once were available only in remote parts of Africa or the south Pacific.

Tropical flowers, in fact, make wonderful wreaths. Although not inclined to dry well, fresh wreaths made from these exotic plants last surprisingly long. And the visual impact is guaranteed to be striking.

Without even realizing it, everyone has ready access to a variety of exotic flowering plants. African violets are available in the plant department of every discount store, and at Christmas, poinsettias can be found everywhere from your local florist to your neighborhood grocery store. Mail-order

businesses and some local nurseries carry the more popular varieties of orchids and other tropicals, and less common plants can be obtained from specialty growers.

If you're interested in trying to cultivate tropical flowers, you'll be joining a trend that began hundreds of years ago. Throughout history people have built special rooms in their homes, and even elaborate buildings, to house unusual, nonnative plants and flowers. In 17th-century England, citrus fruits were grown in long, multiple-windowed rooms called "orangeries," and many an upper-class Victorian home had a conservatory. Today home greenhouses and sunrooms are once again enormously popular, and there are large numbers of hobbyists who enjoy cultivating a variety of tropicals, especially orchids.

Home greenhouses offer the perfect opportunity to recreate the exact conditions needed for tropical plants to prosper, but they're not the only way to meet the task. With just a few minor modifications, your normal home environment can readily accommodate exotic plants. Daylight from nearby windows or sunlight-balanced artificial bulbs can satisfy the plant's need for sun. To offset the overly dry conditions in most homes, particularly in winter, place the pots on gravel-filled trays containing water, and give them a regular misting. Last but not least, don't relegate your plant to a stuffy corner; give it plenty of air circulation, but don't expose it to chilly drafts.

Hardly modest in scale, the globe-shaped blooms of proteas are fist-sized or larger. Their sun-drenched colors when fresh reflect their tropical places of origin—mainly South Africa and Australia. In the wild, proteas are shrubs or small trees that reach as high as 12 feet (3.6 m).

A tropical vine base makes an excellent setting for these beauties. To provide moisture to the flowers and foliage, hot-glue and wire a caged oasis to the top of the base. After cutting the stems to varying lengths (each with a sharp point), insert four fresh "pin cushion" proteas into the oasis. Arrange them asymmetrically, and fill in the sides with pieces of berried eucalyptus, lamb's ears, and a few bits of variegated pittosporum. Then position two dried "pink mink" proteas: a short-stemmed bloom at the top, and one with a longer stem at the side. For added drama, weave a metallic ribbon into the arrangement, hot-gluing it at several spots.

A TROPICAL AMERICAN PLANT, the anthurium is as exotic in appearance as it is in origin. Also called the flamingo flower or heart flower, this plant resembles a calla lily or a jack-in-the-pulpit in its form. The leathery, heart-shaped portion is actually a leaflike structure called a spathe. The long, pink spike in the center contains a multitude of tiny flowers. This tough-looking flower will last up to three weeks after being cut but does not successfully dry.

On a purchased base made of tropical vines and roots, these miniature anthuriums look right at home. Two of the blossoms are inserted into one floral tube, and the third into another. A few stems of papyrus (umbrella plant) are included in the tubes with the flowers. Miniature bouquets of dried genestra are picked into the wreath in a semicircular pattern, with bunches of pepperberries added near the middle. A multi-colored raffia bow adds the finishing touch

*U*BIQUITOUS *at the holiday season, poinsettias hardly seem exotic. (Of course, this is easily recalled if you try to maintain the plant for longer than one season.) They're natives of Mexico but have readily naturalized in other tropical climates including southern Florida. What we generally think of as the flowers are actually brightly colored leaves. The true flowers are the small, berrylike blossoms in the center.*

Given a moist place to tuck its stem, a poinsettia blossom will last beautifully for days. This holiday wreath starts with a large basket-weave base made of grapevine that is sprayed with white paint to give it the look of white wicker. The interior space is filled with Spanish moss, and to sustain the flowers, chunks of well-soaked oasis are wired into the base at convenient locations. Once the poinsettias are arranged in a pleasing crescent, stems of ivy are twined into the open spaces. To keep it from wilting, make sure the ivy is also inserted into the oasis. A seasonal bow, some gilded okra pods, and a few stems of preserved cedar complete the arrangement.

ONE OF THE MOST BEQUILING *of all floral scents belongs to freesia, a native of South Africa. Its elegant, horn-shaped blossoms are found in white and shades of pink, yellow, orange, red, and violet. A spring-blooming bulb, it can easily be forced indoors and makes an excellent cut flower. To grow the plants successfully outdoors, you must have dry summers and cool, moist winters with temperatures not below 20°F (-7°C). For indoor cultivation, freesias need plenty of space for their gangling stems and leaves and, like all bulbs, they must be permitted to rest after blooming.*

Nothing could be more cheerful than this simple arrangement of freesias. Start by cutting several stems with sharp, pointed ends, and insert these so the blossoms cover the top two-thirds of the base. Between the freesias, add stems of deep royal purple statice and pieces of berried eucalyptus. Then fill in the bottom quadrant with tufts of ming fern. If the base can be seen from any perspective, tuck in bits of Spanish moss, and secure them with floral pins.

LEPTOSPERMUM SCOPARIUM, *commonly called "lepto" by florists and growers, is generous with its beauty. A multitude of deep rose blossoms graces each branch. This variety of leptospermum is a native of New Zealand, where it is an evergreen shrub or small tree. There it grows in sun or light shade, and its fine, small-leaved foliage make it a light-textured accent shrub.*

With its delicate blooms and needlelike foliage, a handful of lepto branches form a heavenly corona on a moss-covered wreath. Start with a thoroughly soaked oasis ring, and cover it entirely with sheet moss. Position the lepto branches so they radiate out from the top center. Then enhance the rose theme with a few carefully placed matching carnations. Scatter small clusters of German statice among the flowers to highlight their bright color.

COMPLETELY ATYPICAL of most flowers, the bird-of-paradise (Strelitzia reginae) originated in South Africa. It was considered such a distinctive flower when it was introduced in England, it was named in honor of the queen (reginae). A spear-shaped sheath that grows perpendicular to the stem holds the flowers, which usually emerge one or two at a time. To release them manually, loosen the opening on the head, working from the base to the tip with both index fingers. Then gradually loosen back toward the base with both fingers, and grasp the "birds," popping them out. Once they're out of the base sheath, you can array the flowers artistically.

A flower as unusual as the bird-of-paradise deserves a setting equally unconventional. In this dramatic wreath, melaleuca bark is glued onto a pentagonal foam base. Insert the birds-of-paradise together with a few miniature schefflera leaves and clusters of golden asters into a bouquet holder wired to the base. Add a few stems of curly willow and a lichen-covered branch held in place with large "hairpins" fashioned from heavy-gauge wire. If the bouquet holder is visible, glue pieces of sheet moss over it.

121

ORCHIDS (there are several genera) are considered to be among the most exotic of all flowers, yet they are native to every continent in the world except Antarctica. The 20,000 or so species that make up the orchid family have evolved innumerable methods, some quite complex, for assuring their pollination and reproduction. One of the most fascinating aspects of orchids is that no two plants produce identical flowers.

In their native habitat, a large majority of orchids are epiphytes (air plants) and can be found growing among the branches of trees. This wreath reflects that natural setting, using a vine base as a backdrop for three snowy white Phalaenopsis blossoms. The blooms, once cut from the main branch, have very short stems. It is possible to use a small floral tube to hold the stems, but you may find that method unworkable. If so, wrap a piece of moist cotton around the stem and secure it with floral tape. This is a technique used by florists to construct corsages, and the moisture will support the bloom for several hours. Include one or two galax leaves with each orchid to provide a strong color contrast. To secure the floral tube or taped cotton to the wreath, use a small amount of hot glue. Finish the arrangement with a few stems of berried eucalyptus.

CONTRIBUTING DESIGNERS

BARBARA APPLEBAUM, *together with her husband Lewis, owns and operates Brush Creek Gardens in Fairview, North Carolina. Their flowers are all organically grown in their 1-1/2-acre garden, then air dried. Barbara was formerly an art teacher and florist, and now enjoys making special order craft items. (Pages 41, 93, 94)*

NORA BLOSE *is an herbalist who learned her trade at the knee of her aunt, a country doctor and midwife. She cultivates many of the herbs and flowers that she uses to make craft items sold through her design studio, Nora's Follies, in Candler, North Carolina. (Pages 66, 72, 109, front cover)*

CLARA A. CURTIS *is a consultant to the North Carolina Arboretum, where she previously worked as the greenhouse manager. Her training is in horticultural science and landscape design, and she attributes her artistic abilities to a talented mother and many years of practice. She lives in Clyde, North Carolina. (Pages 5, 27, 84, 91, 110)*

JANE DICUS *owns Dutch Cove Herbs and Everlastings in Winston-Salem, North Carolina. In addition to being a full-time teacher, she dries all of the materials she uses for her wreaths. Her business, which started as a "seat-of-the-britches" operation ten years ago, now takes her to craft shows from Washington, DC to Charleston, SC. (Pages 61, 63, 69, 77, 127)*

JANET FRYE *is the owner of the Enchanted Florist in Arden, North Carolina, where she enjoys using natural materials to create dramatic effects with her floral arrangements. A floral designer for 16 years, Janet loves to share her knowledge of flowers, design techniques, and tips for handling wayward materials. (Pages 8, 29, 30, 35, 38, 39, 45, 46, 51, 52, 59, 64, 80, 82, 87, 101, 105, 118, 121, 128)*

CYNTHIA GILLOOLY *owns and operates The Golden Cricket in Asheville, North Carolina. Previously the owner of Weeds 'n' Things in Sanibel Island, Florida, she has applied her unique and artistic vision to floral design for 13 years. Her passion is to use natural materials in somewhat unconventional arrangements. (Pages 44, 47, 48, 103, 112, 113, 116, 117, 119, 120, 122)*

JEANNETTE HAFNER *grows the flowers and greenery for her designs in her gardens in Orange, Connecticut. She teaches flower drying and arranging techniques as well as design classes. (Pages 2, 28, 32, 37, 58, 60, 62, 65, 75, 85, 111)*

ALYCE NADEAU *grows a wide variety of culinary and decorative herbs at her farm, Goldenrod Mountain Herbs, in Deep Gap, North Carolina. Unlike many commercial growers, she plants her herbs in decorative gardens, which are open to the public in August each year. She markets her herbal creations at trade shows and area farmers' markets. (Pages 26, 33, 40, 68, 71, 76, 81, 90, 95, 102, 104)*

BETH STICKLE *is the proprietor of Bloomin' Art in Asheville, North Carolina. Beth specializes in creating natural designs with fresh and dried flowers, and she enjoys mixing native flowers together with more commonly seen cultivated varieties. (Pages 34, 50, 67, 70, 106, 108)*

And thanks to . . .

PATTI HILL *(pages 86, 92), SANDY MUSH HERB NURSERY (pages 49, 100), TOMMY WALLEN (pages 36, 74), and DIANE WEAVER (page 88, back cover).*

BUTTERY YELLOW BUTTONS of santolina contrast nicely with slender spires of blue salvia. They are joined by white strawflowers, annual statice, and mountain mint leaves, all hot-glued onto a ring covered with German statice.

ACKNOWLEDGMENTS

For their invaluable assistance with location photography, sincere thanks to ROBIN CAPE at Preservation Hall in Asheville, North Carolina; NED GIBSON at B.B. Barns, Inc. in Asheville, North Carolina; ED INGLE at the North Carolina Department of Transportation; JOYCE OWENS at Owens Orchids in Pisgah Forest, North Carolina; SANDRA SOTO at Native Expressions in Asheville, North Carolina; and DIANE WEAVER at Gourmet Gardens in Weaverville, North Carolina.

Warmest thanks to those who opened their homes and gardens to our camera: ELSPETH and JAMES MCCLURE CLARKE, ELFRIDA and WORTH FRADY, and GLADYS and CHARLES LOOMIS.

Wreath at right: A loosely wound grapevine base provides just the right touch—casual yet elegant—for an armful of garden flowers. The blossoms include blue hydrangeas, zinnias, marigolds, veronica, yarrow, and native larkspur. Short stems of artemisia leaves provide the greenery. Flowers and foliage are kept fresh by three well-soaked bouquet holders wired onto the base.

INDEX